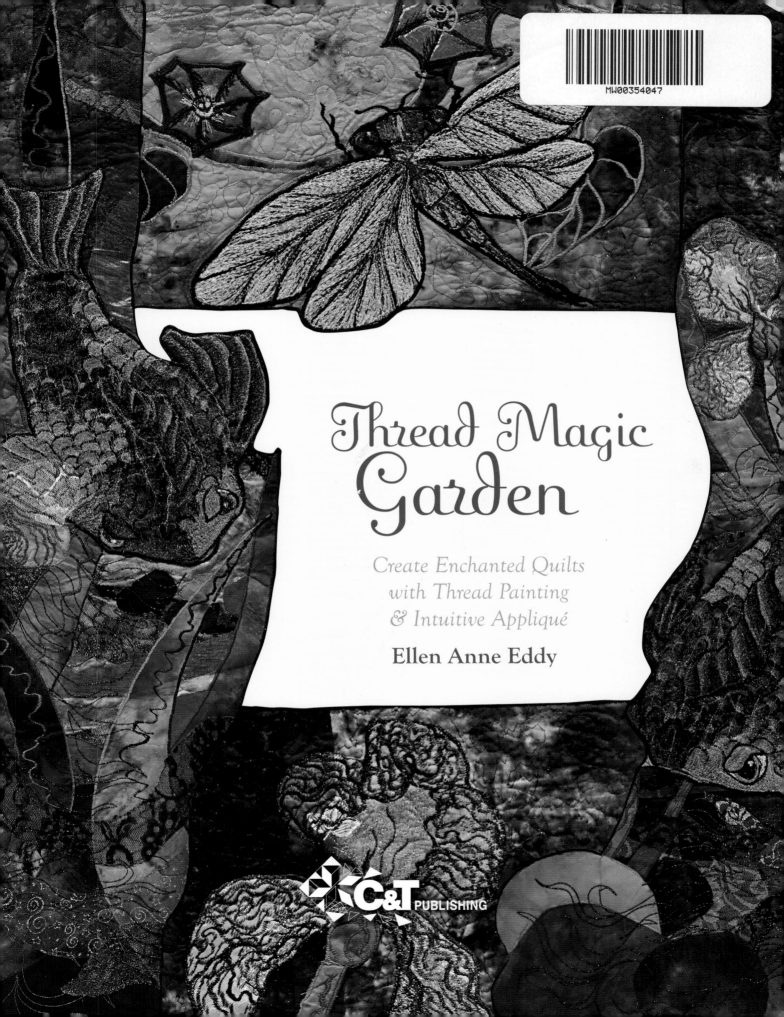

Thread Magic Garden

Create Enchanted Quilts
with Thread Painting
& Intuitive Appliqué

Ellen Anne Eddy

C&T PUBLISHING

Text and Photography copyright © 2012 by Ellen Anne Eddy

Photography and Artwork copyright © 2012 by C&T Publishing, Inc.

Publisher: Amy Marson

Creative Director: Gailen Runge

Acquisitions Editor: Susanne Woods

Editors: Karla Menaugh and Cynthia Bix

Technical Editor: Carolyn Aune

Cover Designer: April Mostek

Book Designer: Kerry Graham

Production Coordinator: Jenny Davis

Production Editor: S. Michele Fry

Illustrator: Zinnia Heinzmann

Photography by Christina Carty-Francis and Diane Pedersen
of C&T Publishing, Inc., unless otherwise noted

Published by C&T Publishing, Inc., P.O. Box 1456, Lafayette, CA 94549

Library of Congress Cataloging-in-Publication Data

Eddy, Ellen Anne, 1953-

 Thread magic garden : create enchanted quilts with thread painting &
intuitive appliqué / Ellen Anne Eddy.

    p. cm.

ISBN 978-1-60705-261-6 (soft cover)

1. Embroidery, Machine. 2. Machine quilting. I. Title.

TT772.E335 2012

746.44028--dc23

                          2011019329

Printed in China

10 9 8 7 6 5 4 3 2

Acknowledgments

This book stretched my own abilities, and I found myself leaning on a number of people to build my expertise and help me out.

Special thanks to Lauren Strach, who helped so much with photos, inspiration, and eye. Thanks to her daughter, Anna, who was my fabulous hand model. Dan Bruin, from Bruin Studio, generously tutored me in photography. Chesterton Feed and Gardens were gracious about letting me stalk their nursery with a camera in hand. Thanks also to my proofreaders, Melida Boman, Rebecca Brown, Kathy Semone, Zinnia Fiddes, Yolonda Kleinhans, Joan Breece, and Jennifer Gordon, who helped shape the book with their excellent comments.

Dedication

For Mary Annis, my best mentor and friend, and to everyone who has walked me through their garden or walked through mine.

Contents

Through the Garden Gate

There's something about a garden. It's our first idea of paradise, our Eden, our place of rest and recuperation.

Almost all gardens are framed by their flowers. They adorn the memories of loves lost and found. Our lives are a construction of flowers given and taken, of gardens kept, visited, walked, picked, and left to bloom and fade.

My earliest garden memory is trading my childhood fistful of dandelions to my neighbor for a bouquet of moss roses. I adored their bright oranges and fuchsias. We picked flowers for neighbors on May Day. On my birthday, lilacs were my gift from the yard. We celebrated July 4th with the daylily my father brought from his mother's house. Years later, after living so long in apartments, I realized that I had forgotten what it was like to have flowers and to measure time by flowers bloomed and spent.

So it took me by surprise to learn that when I'd bought a house, I'd also bought a garden. I was uncontrollable. I had to make this strange place my own. I filled in one patch after another, covering every stray inch with blooms, flowering shrubs, and weeping trees.

Then fall came and I could barely look at the strange, dead, brown land. So I went into my studio and began my own garden in sheers and hand-dyed fabrics.

Now I tend both my inner and outer gardens, and I watch myself bloom with my blossoms. The seasons within the studio are jumbled, but the growing conditions are just right!

Photo by Lauren Strach

Floral Arrangement 25, 15" × 39"
by Ellen Anne Eddy, 2008; owned by
Glacier Quilts, Kalispell, Montana

Observation

The Garden of the Heart

My garden intoxicates me. The sights and smells, textures and sounds are my daily retreat. Just as I slip into the garden, the garden slips into my quilts. But I don't find it as easy to draw flowers as I do frogs. Flowers elude me when I approach them with paper and pencil.

Years ago, my mother taught me to cut shapes instead. She was a schoolteacher, and one of the banes of her life was her bulletin board. She swore she couldn't draw. Instead, she cut shapes and letters that made a great graphic display.

Butterfly Garden, 27″ × 59″, by Ellen Anne Eddy, 2010

What Does a Flower Look Like?

Photo by Lauren Strach

Verbal memory won't give us the information we need to create a bloom like this. We need a photograph, a visual reference.

The standard quilter's answer to avoid drawing is to find a pattern or a drawing to copy. But those images offer a limited world. No matter how beautifully they're rendered, they are always someone else's vision. You also have to be sensitive to copyright issues.

I will show you how to take several approaches to building flowers without patterns and without limits. The process starts with some careful observation. The key is to simplify each flower into easy-to-cut shapes that can be used to build a flower petal by petal or as a background for stitchery blooms.

You can stimulate your visual memory by examining each flower. How big is the center? What angle are the petals? Without actively looking, it's difficult to know.

So begin your quest. Bring in some flowers from the garden. Buy yourself a bouquet. Get your camera. Or start with those wonderful catalogs from the seed and bulb companies. Add some lovely photographic books. Don't neglect the fabulous drawings and photos in children's books. Silk flowers, blooms that last forever, can also inspire us. You are very welcome to use my photography and drawings to begin your journey.

VIEWPOINTS

Everything changes with your point of view. If you look down on a flower, you see more of the center and the stamens and the front side of the petals.

Direct face shot of cosmos

If you're looking from the back, the sepal will show instead. You also will see the backside of the petals and more of the leaves and stems, but no center.

The back of a cosmos shows completely different elements.

Floral Canopy 2, 10″ × 13″, by Ellen Anne Eddy, 2010

SHAPES

Saucer

The cosmos makes a perfect saucer. Petals radiate out from the center in a saucer shape. The basic flower parts are all the same: Petals form around the center and join in back at the sepal. Though saucer flowers do have stamens, they're usually too small to be obvious.

Daisies, asters, dandelions, calendula, and coneflower are all saucer flowers.

Cup

The petals of cup flowers also radiate from the center. The petals form a cup, and the stamens and pistil are visible.

Lily from the front

There is no sepal in the back. In lilies, tulips, and daylilies, the cup is made of petals that join in the back.

Lily from the back

Bell

In bell shapes, like Canterbury bells, Japanese lanterns, lilies of the valley, and hostas, the cup is a single-petal shape with the sepal at the back. The flowers are made with many blooms, but each is a single, separate petal.

Canterbury bells viewed from the side

Ball of Blooms

Finally, some flowers are just balls of blooms. Phlox, verbena, alliums, lilacs, and hydrangea are ball shapes of smaller flowers.

Phlox viewed from above

Cup and Saucer

Some flowers have both a cup and a saucer. Sometimes the cup is on the saucer. This daffodil has a saucer made of external petals and a cup made from one petal shape.

Daffodil at three-quarter view

Morning glories and calla lilies have a saucer that rims around the cup.

Photo by Lauren Strach

Morning glory

Approaches to Building Flowers

OUTER SHAPES

You can construct many flowers by cutting their outer shapes from fabric and creating the petals from stitching. I love this simple, playful approach. You can transform the shapes into flowers by making a center for the flower and then segmenting and ornamenting the outer edges to make petals. Even if your flower is a total fantasy, the eye will recognize it as a flower.

Detail of *Duet* (page 103)—This iris is constructed with loop shapes.

COMPONENTS

You also can create blooms from the flower components, petal by petal and leaf by leaf. To see some samples, see Planning Flowers from Elements (page 70).

Using this technique, you can create very recognizable flowers. But there's no reason to be caught in reality if it's not to your taste. You may not have blue roses in your garden, but you can create them for your quilt. You can have flowers of impossible shapes, colors, and sizes. There are no bad flowers. How could there be? However, you should probably be consistent in terms of certain choices within your bouquets: Are you being realistic or not? Where is your viewpoint? Is your design abstract or focused? It helps to make up your mind.

Daylilies come in an endless variety. You can't choose wrong.

Photos by Lauren Strach

Color Theory for Flowers

Color choices are always personal, but some basic considerations can help you.
It helps to know enough color theory to confidently pick the colors you need.

The Color Wheel

The color wheel maps the relationships of colors. Knowledge of the color wheel
gives you an excellent place to start making color choices.

HUES

Hues are the colors themselves. The
color wheel places them in relation-
ship to one other. For example, related
to the jewel-tone color wheel are the
many variations in value, clarity, and
temperature of the hues.

Jewel-tone hues

VALUE

Value is the darkness or lightness of
colors. Darkened colors, which are
called tones, create opulent colors,
shadows, and undertones. Lightened
colors are called tints. Pale and pastel
tints create highlights, glowing edges,
and delicate transparencies.

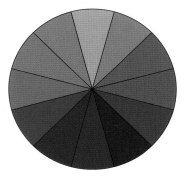

Darkened hues

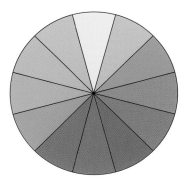

Tinted hues

Detail of *Wisteria Pond* (page 104)—Cooler shades of pink and purple counteract the other warm yellow-green elements in this branch of wisteria.

NEUTRALS

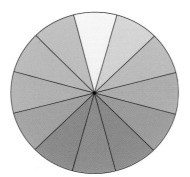

Neutral color wheel

Any color can be toned or tinted into a neutral shade. Neutrals are shades that have no color impact. They are always neutral only in the context of the combination in which they are used. A light periwinkle can become a gray in the right light and context. Likewise, lime acts as the new neutral against a splash of bright reds, oranges, and yellows.

Most colors can be toned or tinted into a neutral shade. Black, white, and brown are also considered neutral colors. All of their contrast is in value—darkness and light.

CLARITY

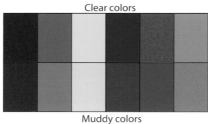

Clear colors

Muddy colors

Colors can be either clear or muddy. Clear tones show objects up close. Muddy colors can indicate objects in a distance, or they can denote the undersides of leaves and petals. The darker, muddier tones at the bottom of a leaf can differentiate the back from the front.

TEMPERATURE

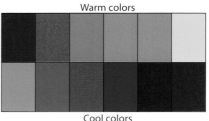

Warm colors

Cool colors

There are two distinctions in color temperature. Red-violet, red, red-orange, orange, yellow-orange, and yellow make up the warm colors. Yellow-green, green, blue-green, blue, blue-violet, and violet make up the cool ones. When we put warm and cool colors together, they create an exciting visual thermal shock.

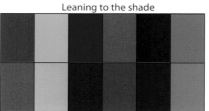

Leaning to the shade

Leaning to the sun

But there's also a subtler form of thermal shock: Most colors lean a bit to the sun or the shade, either warm or cool. Within the color wheel, hues can be cast in different temperatures. If the color is more like the ones on the top row of the picture, it leans toward the shade. If the color is more like the ones on the bottom row, it leans toward the sun.

Detail of *Daylily Pond* (page 86)—In this quilt placing warm orange flowers against a blue background can create an exciting visual thermal shock.

Color Combinations

MONOCHROMATIC COLOR

Monochromatic purple color range

Monochromatic combinations are made from one hue in different values, dark to light. These colors create quiet, rich combinations without a strong color impact.

COMPLEMENTARY COLORS

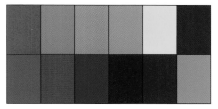

Jewel-tone complements

Complementary colors are opposite each other on the wheel and create the strongest contrasts when used together.

If you think one complementary pair is exciting, try adding more than one. You can even use the whole color wheel in a piece for a maximum effect.

ANALOGOUS COLOR COMBINATIONS

This analogous range creates a flower with rich, full coloration.

Combinations made from an arc of the color wheel are called analogous selections. They can be either cool or warm color arcs or a combination of both. These smooth color combinations are rich and lovely.

SPLIT COMPLEMENTARY COLORS

A split complementary combination includes oranges and yellows contrasted with blue-violet.

A split-complement recipe includes an analogous arc of color plus a complement to one of those colors. The smooth, rich combination with the spark of a complement is an unbeatable, exciting choice.

Creeping through the Charlie, 15" × 15", by Ellen Anne Eddy, 2008; owned by Ann Ribbens

The orange–yellow–blue-violet range is used in the fabric and thread for the sunflower.

Color Decisions within Design

BACKGROUND FABRIC

The background fabric may be the least noticeable color choice in a quilt, but in one way, it is the most important. The background sets the tone of the light in the piece, and that tone defines the colors you use within it.

If you are working on a purple background, that purple will reflect in all the petals. Therefore, you need to choose your fabrics and threads with that purple fabric in mind. The threads also should echo the color. For example, the pastel threads picked for the flower reflect the purple tones of the background.

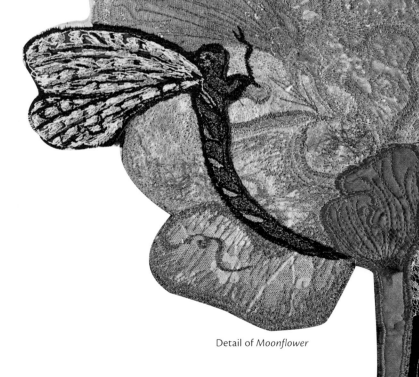

Detail of *Moonflower*

Moonflower, 11″ × 44″, by Ellen Anne Eddy, 2008

The dark purple background sets the tone for the entire quilt.

Choosing a less natural-colored background almost immediately begins to abstract your work. However, there's something exciting about a fuchsia sky or an orange moon. There's no reason not to be wild.

The amount of contrast between your background and your flower fabric choices sets the scene for either subtle ornamental petals or screaming floral wonders. Well-chosen, high-contrast color combinations will make your flowers glow like gems in your floral garden.

Detail of *Lady Mantis 2* (page 62)—The white hosta flower, stitched in pale crystals, blues, and greens, glows against a fuchsia sky.

FLOWER FABRIC

To create a vital design, you need variety in your fabrics. A range of any hue, including dark and light, will give you variation as well as a sense of dimension.

If you choose flower colors that mimic or blend with your background, your choices will be more subtle and delicate. If you make choices that contrast flower and background, then your work will be more active and robust. Neither is right or wrong; both are simple ways to show your point of view.

Tip ....
Collect color combinations that make your heart flutter. If you see a picture or have paint chips of colors that you like together, keep track of the combinations you love and use them.
....

Courtship Rituals 6, 18″ × 22″, by Ellen Anne Eddy, 2004; owned by Melida Boman

A bit of green stitching shocks and shades the center of this red flower.

Shockers and Shaders

Most color ranges will be livelier if you include both a shocker and a shader. A shocker color jolts the other colors by providing a high-contrast value against the rest of the range. It adds energy to the combination. Shader colors give a sense of dimension and weight to any combination.

Complementary colors always add drama to flowers. For that reason, they're excellent and exciting shockers. Tertiary colors—yellow-orange, red-orange, blue-green, yellow-green, red-violet, and blue-violet—are also great shockers. They blend well while also electrifying the basic color.

A shadow is always an excuse for purple. But don't forget the darker tone of a flower's complementary color—dark green, brown, burgundy, and blue. They all work well as shadows.

Floral Arrangement 26, 16" × 16", by Ellen Anne Eddy, 2006

A wild range of thread colors combine in a fantasy flower that is basically just bright.

Dos and Don'ts

Dos and Don'ts

Do decide which edge of your flower is darker or lighter. Consistency throughout the work matters more than the decision itself. Are the inner petals lighter? Darker? Are the outer petals duller? Make your decision based on where the light is in your background, and stick with it for a focused effect.

Do use a wide-enough range of color to make it work. Choose at least a light, a dark, a medium, a shocker, and a shader. For larger flowers, go much darker and much lighter than your first choice because the eye will blend it all, and add more colors in between.

Don't use big blocks of just white, unless you're planning to be abstract. You can show shades of white with grays, blues, and pastels. Or consider iridescent whites, silvers, and shades of gold metallic; they will register as white even though they aren't.

DEFINITIVE THREADWORK

Your threadwork will define the color of your flower, while the fabrics simply offer a tone. The thread outlining and shading will make all the difference.

I work with both metallic and polyester embroidery threads. The polyester threads offer a bright, intense color with a soft sheen. The metallic threads are much more reflective. The effect is more textural and the colors are less intense.

THREADS

The same color considerations work for thread, though thread brings something special to the table. Because a strand of thread is so small, you can add excitement in very bright, dark, or contrasted bits. Don't be afraid to go much brighter, lighter, or darker than you think might work. The delicacy of 40-weight thread gives you just a dash of extra color and permits you to be bolder.

Detail of *Floral Arrangement 25* (page 6)

Bright blue and violet shockers rock this orange and yellow bloom.

Choosing Materials and Tools

Using the right materials and tools can make your sewing life easier. Here are the ones I use. For ordering information, see Resources (page 111).

Fabric

Hand-dyed fabric   I dye nearly all the cotton fabric in my quilts. I use sponge dyeing, which allows me to build a landscape and light source into each background fabric, as well as special characteristics into fabrics used for flowers and creatures. I also dye cheesecloth and embroidery threads. For more information, see About the Author (page 110).

Commercial fabrics   I use a variety of laces, organzas, lamés, sheers, brocades, and embroidered fabrics. Warning: Avoid knitted fabrics; they neither piece nor fuse well.

Threads

Polyester 40-weight machine embroidery thread   You also could use either cotton or rayon thread, but both will break more often than polyester. And I like polyester thread for its beautiful sheen.

Metallic machine embroidery thread   This thread comes in a range of colors. Madeira Supertwist and Superior metallic threads are my favorites.

Sliver thread   My favorite thread for stippling, sliver thread is a shiny, flat thread that comes in many colors and can be used in the bobbin.

Monofilament thread   When I want a soft edge on an appliqué shape, I use clear for light colors and smoke for dark colors.

Fusible Webbing and Adhesives

Repositionable fusible webbing   I like Steam-A-Seam 2 (by The Warm Company) because I can pat the webbing on the fabric, cut out shapes, and work on my design, all without using the iron.

Spray adhesive   OESD 505 Spray and Fix adhesive spray is an option for attaching the fabric background to polyester felt in the stabilizer sandwich. See Stabilizer Sandwich (page 19).

Stabilizers

Stiff tear-away stabilizer   I slip a piece of Pellon Stitch-n-Tear under my stabilizer sandwich fabric before I start sewing.

Nonwoven stabilizer   For stitching directly on the background fabric, I use midweight Hydro-Stick by OESD or an iron-on stiff nonwoven interfacing.

Dissolvable stabilizer   I use OESD AquaFilm Wash-Away Topping embroidery stabilizer for thread globbing. For more information, see Thread Globbing (page 26).

Felt

Polyester felt   This makes a great stabilizer, as well as a great quilt bat for wallhangings. It's 60″ wide, does not fray, and is an excellent stabilizer for either the quilt surface or the appliqué elements. I use either 505 Spray and Fix to attach a quilt surface or Steam-A-Seam 2 to attach appliqué elements. Then I use a tear-away nonwoven interfacing underneath to keep the embroidery crisp.

Presser Feet

Darning foot   For machine embroidery and free-motion appliqué, use the smallest foot that clears your widest stitch width. Smaller darning feet give you the best-supported stitch.

Straight/zigzag stitching foot   This versatile foot can be used for couching.

Buttonhole foot with a two-channel escape   The grooves in the bottom of this foot allow room for the thick stitching in my corded buttonhole binding. See Binding Quilts with Irregular Edges (page 30).

Other Essentials

Size 90 topstitch needle   I use this needle for all free-motion work. The sharp point gives a fine, straight stitch line and the larger needle eye causes fewer thread breaks.

Hoop   A hoop helps control distortion and gives you something to hold on to while you are moving your fabric. The hoop you see in this book is Sharon Schamber's Quilt Halo, a one-piece, weighted, rubberized hoop that simply slides across your quilt surface without needing to be clamped. This tool slashes my sewing time because I don't have to constantly rehoop. To give you enough support, your hoop should be no more than 9″ wide.

Stitch Essentials

Just the shapes of flowers can be exciting. Creating a design with simple fabric shapes is an easy way to make abstract flowers as a design effect (see Observation, page 7). But it's so much more fun to also stitch the flowers. Both straight-stitch and zigzag free-motion embroidery are powerful drawing tools.

Straight stitch allows you to add detail to or to fill in your sketches.

Zigzag stitching is the backbone of flower work. I love doing free-motion zigzag because of the range and possibility of expression it gives me. It's fabulous!

The free-motion zigzag stitch is fluid. It changes not in terms of stitch length or width, but rather in terms of the direction in which you put your fabric through the machine.

Stitching also allows you to shade your flowers in a million ways. A line of thread is so small that all kinds of far-too-bright colors can dance across the surface to create the petals you want. Like all wonderful art tools, its benefit becomes greater with a bit of practice.

Setting Up the Machine

- Drop the feed dogs. Once you have dropped your feed dogs, the stitch length is defined by how you physically move your fabric through the machine. Therefore, the machine's stitch-length setting is not relevant.

- Decrease the top tension slightly. The top thread should pull slightly to the backside of your work.

- Use the smallest foot that clears your widest stitch width. Smaller darning feet give you a better-supported stitch.

- Thread the machine correctly. The presser foot position not only raises and lowers the foot but also opens and closes the tension disks. Always thread the machine with the presser foot up so that the tension disks are open. Always sew with the foot down so that the tension disks are engaged. Always start by bringing the bottom thread up to the top, as this keeps the thread from knotting on the bobbin side.

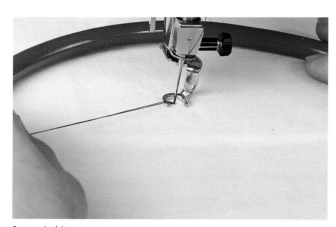

Start stitching

Flower created in straight stitch

The Tension Headache Cure ....

Some tension headaches can't be cured by anything over the counter. But by following these rules, you can at least alleviate most of your machine tension headaches.

- When in doubt, rethread the machine top and bobbin. Thread sometimes pops out of tension. Nine times out of ten, rethreading will fix the problem.

- If you're working from the front of your fabric, decrease the top tension slightly.

- If you're working from the back, increase the top tension slightly.

- New day, new needle. New project, new needle. Also change your needle if you're getting thread breakage.

- Clean and oil your machine. Check your manual to learn how to clean your machine and where to oil. Some machines don't need to be oiled, but they all need to be cleaned regularly. I suggest a thorough cleaning after every third bobbin.

....

Stabilizer Sandwich

Stabilizer sandwich

All intense embroidery needs stabilization to function. Make a stabilizer sandwich to support your most obsessive embroidery. This is a good idea for heavy straight-stitch embroidery; it is essential for larger zigzag work.

MATERIALS

For more information about my recommendations, see Choosing Materials and Tools (page 17). For ordering information, see Resources (page111).

- 11″ × 11″ square of fabric to match your quilt's background fabric

- Double-sided fusible webbing

- Polyester felt (any color)

- Stiff tear-away stabilizer

- Spray adhesive (optional)

- Pins or tacks and tack tool

1. Layer your sandwich in this order from top to bottom:

- Background fabric

- Double-sided fusible webbing

- Polyester felt

2. Iron the sandwich so that the background fabric, fusible webbing, and felt are fused together.

Note

For lighter support, you can substitute repositionable spray glue for the fusible webbing. It does not require ironing, but it also does not stabilize the piece as much.

3. Slip the stabilizer sheet underneath the sandwich before you start to sew.

4. Cut the component shapes for your particular flower. See Planning Flowers from Simple Shapes (page 48). Fuse the flower components onto the top of the sandwich and embellish them with stitches. Embroider directly onto the sandwich.

5. Cut out around the flower, cutting away the puckered and distorted background.

6. Slip another stabilizer sheet underneath your quilt's background fabric. Place the embroidered flower on top and appliqué it to the background fabric with a free-motion zigzag stitch. For more on how to stitch your flower to the background, see Free-Motion Appliqué (page 24).

Stitch Lessons

MATERIALS AND TOOLS

For more information about my recommendations, see Choosing Materials and Tools (page 17). For ordering information, see Resources (page 111).

- 9″ × 9″ square of muslin (You will be able to see what you're doing better on plain muslin, but any quilt-weight cotton will work.)

- 9″ × 9″ piece of nonwoven iron-on stabilizer

- Polyester 40-weight embroidery thread

- Size 90 topstitch needle

- Hoop

Note

When making practice pieces, it is simpler and more economical to layer just muslin and the nonwoven iron-on stabilizer, rather than using all the layers needed to make a stabilizer sandwich for a finished piece.

ZIGZAG STITCH

Almost all the effects I create are made from a combination of the following stitches. I outline the edge of the petal and then shade and smooth it with the same color thread. Then I go to the other edge of the petal and repeat the process with another thread color. Finally, I doodle a line through the center to create a dimple in the petal.

Free-motion zigzag stitching makes it possible to switch from one stitch to another simply by changing the direction of your motion.

I usually set the stitch width to 4 on a scale of 0 to 5. Remember, the stitch width changes as you change the way you move your fabric through the sewing machine. The faster you move your hands, the larger the stitch length. The faster you run your machine, the smaller the stitch length. Move your hands very slowly to get a smooth, covering edge.

Free-motion zigzag is defined not so much by the width or length of the stitch but by the angle at which you feed the fabric through the machine. Almost all free-motion embellishment is created by a combination of three angles—straight out to the side, at a slant, or straight ahead. Stitching in a circular motion adds the versatile garnet stitch.

Zigzag stitching at different angles

By combining the following seven very different stitches, you can create and highlight almost any shape:

- Sideways connecting stitch
- Sideways fill-in stitch
- Slanted outline stitch
- Slanted shading stitch
- Smoothing stitch
- Bulky outline stitch
- Garnet stitch

Detail of *Floral Canopy 2* (page 8)—The different zigzag stitches make these petals stand out from each other.

Stitching Straight Out to the Side

SIDEWAYS CONNECTING STITCH

If you move the fabric 90° out to the side, you will get a pencil-thin horizontal line. These thin lines can pass through a color area with almost no impact. Use them to travel from one area to another.

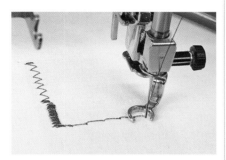
Move the stitching from side to side.

SIDEWAYS FILL-IN STITCH

In the example, I used the connecting stitch as free-standing fill-in. However, you also can attach it to one side of an outline. This stitch makes a fast fill-in that can be used to build up color or to shade an area.

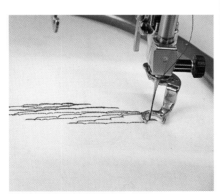
Sideways fill-in stitch

Stitching at a Slant

SLANTED OUTLINE STITCH

Move the fabric at a 40° to 60° angle through the machine. This stitch makes a line like a calligraphy pen. Not only does this make a great outline, but it also does a beautiful appliqué edge for curved images.

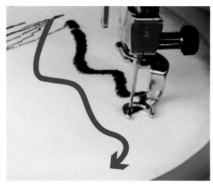
Slanted outline stitch

With this stitch, be sure to keep a consistent angle. Move the angle of the fabric to follow the outline. If you need to stitch in a different direction, turn the piece 180° to keep the stitch angle consistent.

SLANTED SHADING STITCH

Move the fabric back and forth as you stitch, following one side of the outline stitching and keeping the 40° to 60° angle. This creates a thread fill-in that connects to the outline and that shades or texturizes the appliqué edge.

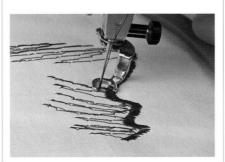
Shading an outline

Stitching Straight Ahead

SMOOTHING STITCH

Run a straight line of zigzag stitching between the fill-in and the outline to smooth the connection between them, creating a visual whole.

Smoothing an outline

BULKY OUTLINE STITCH

If you move the fabric very slowly, the zigzag fills in a nearly solid line, creating a hard, blocky outline suitable for buildings, sidewalks, and hard mechanical lines.

Stitching in Circles

GARNET STITCH

To make this stitch, move your hands in a circle. This versatile stitch can be used as texture, outline, or fill. You can make variations of it by stitching in spirals.

Garnet zigzag stitch

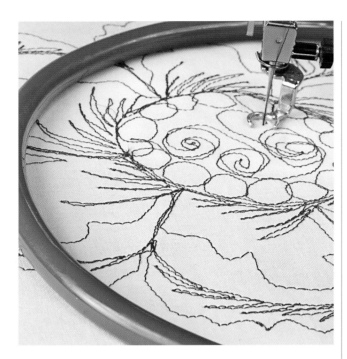

Drawing a Flower in Straight Stitch

Straight-stitch, free-motion sketching can go in any direction. You will have more success if you move your hands quickly. Until you are comfortable doing freehand machine sketching, you can lightly draw your design in pencil.

1. Set up your sewing machine as you did for zigzag stitching, but set the stitch width to 0. (See Setting Up the Machine, page 18.)

2. Draw a circle for the flower center. Then use the garnet stitch to make a frame of small circles around the flower.

3. Draw petals around the center.

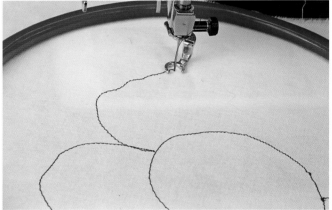

Larger flower petals

4. Edge the flowers with a ruffled echo stitch.

Ruffled echo stitch

5. Use a faux zigzag stitch for shading. Zigzag stitching is made for shading. However, sometimes using a straight stitch works better because it creates less distortion. Just move the stitching back and forth to create a faux zigzag stitch.

STRAIGHT STITCH

The straight stitch creates a simple line that is like drawing with a pencil, except that here, you're moving the "paper" while your machine holds the "pencil." This stitch creates a delicate line that is perfect for detailing and defining images.

Move your hands faster in straight stitch than you did for the zigzag stitch.

In addition to sketching the outline with a straight stitch, you also can use small repetitive movements to create and fill in your flower. By practicing the following exercises, you can learn how and when to use these stitches:

- Garnet stitch
- Free-motion sketch stitch
- Ruffled echo stitch
- Faux zigzag stitch
- Spiral stitch
- Parallel stitch
- Stippling stitch

Faux zigzag stitch

6. Use another ruffled echo stitch to edge the inner petals.

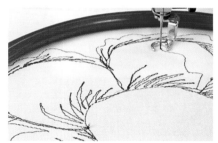

Decorative ruffled echo stitch

7. Fill in the center with the garnet stitch in smaller circles.

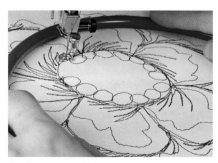

Smaller garnet stitch

8. Use the spiral stitch to fill in the smaller circles.

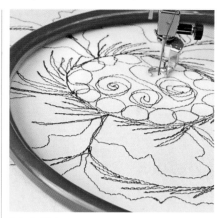

Spiral stitch

9. Use the parallel stitch to fill in the leaf shape.

Parallel lines

10. Use stippling to add texture to the background of a project. Stippling is simply wandering in rhythmic patterns across the surface. There are a million ways to do it and they're all right. You also can sign your name within the stippling. It's a great way to document your quilts.

Stipple signature

Dos and Don'ts

- Do match your stabilizer sandwich fabric to your quilt's surface. If you really want to highlight your flower, you can match its sandwich fabric to the flower color. Either way, a little bit of the sandwich's background fabric will always show through the appliqué stitching.

- Do fuse the sandwich completely. If you don't, your needle will gum up, and you'll get skipped stitches.

- Do put a tear-away stabilizer behind the quilt's background fabric before you do any stitching.

- Do minimize distortion by using the stabilizer sandwich, hoops, and smaller stitch widths.

- Do drop your feed dogs. If you have a machine that doesn't drop its feed dogs, set the stitch length to 0 to keep the feed dogs from moving.

- Do keep track of the angle of your stitch. You need to turn your piece consistently as you stitch in order to create a nice, angled edge.

- Do be patient with your progress. Everything worth doing is worth doing badly at first. Try these stitches without making judgments on your work. Your skill will improve as you keep trying.

- Do move your hands quickly for straight stitching.

- Don't move your hands too fast for zigzag stitching.

- Do move your hands very slowly to get a smooth zigzag to cover the edge.

- Don't sew too slowly. You'll want your machine to sew at its top functional speed. (Some machines break thread at top speed. If your machine does, go only as fast as the thread will allow.)

FREE-MOTION APPLIQUÉ

Use the slanted free-motion zigzag stitch (page 20) to apply flowers and other shapes to the quilt's background fabric.

You can use any stitch width setting. I usually use 4 on a scale of 0 to 5. Choose a stitch just wide enough to cover the appliqué edges.

Soft-Edge Appliqué

Use monofilament nylon thread and open stitches to apply transparent or translucent images or images that shouldn't have a hard edge. Water, air, mist, fire, snow, and some flower petals are more effective without a hard edge. Use clear monofilament thread for pastel or white images. Use smoke-colored thread for anything darker. Stitch quickly around the appliqué so that you make just enough stitches to attach it.

Hard-Edge Appliqué

Most appliqué is done with a hard edge, which creates a visible line for petals, branches, and stems, completely encasing the edges.

The slanted outline stitch (page 21) works well for hard-edged appliqué. Stitch by moving your hands very slowly and the machine very fast. This will create a beautifully covered edge. You can use any 30- to 40-weight embroidery thread.

Garnet stitch, either straight or zigzag, also works well as an appliqué edge. This stitch creates small loops around the shape, giving another dimension to your work. To see an example of the garnet stitch used for appliqué, see the detail of *Jazzed: Encircled* (page 49).

A Case for Working on the Back of the Fabric ....

If you want to follow a drawn design, you can draw it on the stabilizer sheet and work from the back of your project. Put the embroidery thread in the bobbin and turn your project upside down, with the stabilizer sheet on top. Stitch on the back of your project, with all the decorative thread going onto the front from the bobbin.

The benefit: The upper thread goes back and forth through the needle 50 times before it goes into the fabric. Fragile threads break under that abuse, but they can be put in the bobbin and stitched upside down because they get pulled up once with almost no breakage.

....

Detail of *Midnight Stroll* (page 104)—The moon and cloud are outlined in soft-edge appliqué. The flower is outlined in hard-edge appliqué in metallic thread.

SKILL BUILDING:
Special Stitch Techniques

Detail of *Lady Mantis 2* (page 62)
The multicolored moon is made of Angelina fibers.

SKILL BUILDER:
Using Angelina Fiber

Angelina fiber makes some of the most exciting sheer material available. It was used for the moon in *Lady Mantis 2*. This fiber is easy to work with, comes in a huge range of colors, and makes luminous flowers, moons, and suns.

MATERIALS AND TOOLS

For more information about my recommendations, see Choosing Materials and Tools (page 17). For ordering information, see Resources (page 111).

- Angelina or Crystalina fiber with bonding capabilities: Angelina fiber looks like cotton candy. When it is heated, it melts into a glassy sheer fiber that can be applied with fusible webbing or stitching. Crystalina is the same substance, but it is cut coarser. They can be used interchangeably and are available in a variety of colors. Angelina and Crystalina fibers bond only to themselves; they will not bond to fabric or to thread. However, you can trap thread clippings between layers of the fibers.

- Nonstick pressing cloth: You can use parchment paper for this, but a nonstick pressing cloth will help protect the fiber from burning.

- Thread clippings (*optional*)

- Double-sided fusible webbing: You will need a section as large as your fused Angelina piece.

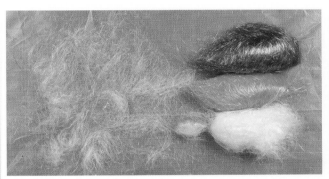

Angelina fiber

1. To make a fiber moon, choose fiber colors to blend and arrange the fibers in a light layer on the pressing cloth.

2. Use the rayon setting on your iron. Fold the pressing cloth over the top of the fibers and use the iron to fuse them.

Ironing Angelina

3. To use the fiber moon, adhere it to double-sided fusible webbing. It will then be ready to appliqué to a stabilizer sandwich or to your quilt backing. (For more on appliquéing shapes, see Stitch Essentials, pages 18–24.)

Fused Angelina fibers

This hosta bloom was made from Angelina fiber that was fused to a stabilizer sandwich and stitched. Then it was cut out and applied to the quilt surface.

Dos and Don'ts ....

■ Do mix Angelina and Crystalina fibers to get the colors you want.

■ Do add machine embroidery thread into the mix. Simply put it between light layers of Angelina fiber to trap it inside the fused fibers.

■ Don't overheat the Angelina. It will burn and turn brown if it is overheated. If you fuse it with Steam-A-Seam 2, be careful not to heat it too much.

■ Don't layer the fiber too thickly, as it won't fuse properly.

....

SKILL BUILDER:
Thread Globbing

If you do machine embroidery, then you probably have lots of thread clippings. Here's a great use for those beautiful bits of thread that you hate to throw away: Glob them onto your quilt. They make great bird's nests, sphagnum moss, stamens, and ground cover.

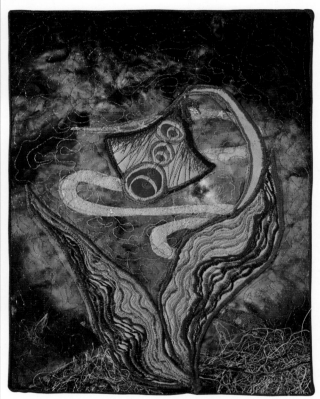
Grotto Gem, 14" × 11", by Ellen Anne Eddy, 2010

Organza in the background gives a misty quality, and globbed thread at the bottom is like brightly colored sphagnum moss.

MATERIALS AND TOOLS

For more information about my recommendations, see Choosing Materials and Tools (page 17). For ordering information, see Resources (page 111).

■ Dissolvable stabilizer

■ Embroidery thread clippings

■ Monofilament threads

■ Spray bottle with water

Pin film over threads.

1. Lay the embroidery threads on the quilt surface and pin dissolvable stabilizer film over them.

2. Using monofilament thread, stitch over the glob of embroidery threads with a straight-stitch garnet stitch. Thoroughly stitch down any loose threads. The stabilizer film keeps the thread from getting caught in your darning foot.

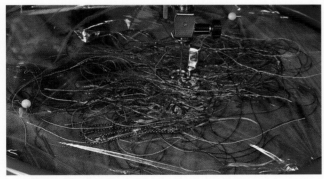

Stitch down film.

3. Spray the surface with water. The water will dissolve the stabilizer, leaving the thread stitched in place.

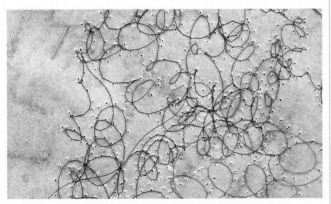

The back of the globbing shows how dense the garnet stitching needs to be to hold the thread in place.

SKILL BUILDER:
Machine Beading

Detail of *Three-Point Landing* (page 85)—The dark blue seed beads punctuate the centers of these bright blooms.

Many flowers are more exciting with beaded centers. Machine beading is quick and easy.

MATERIALS AND TOOLS

For more information about my recommendations, see Choosing Materials and Tools (page 17). For ordering information, see Resources (page 111).

- Monofilament thread

- Size 5 to 8 seed beads
  (The larger beads are easier to handle.)

- Hoop

- Stiff tear-away stabilizer

- Size 90 topstitching needle

SETTING UP

1. Thread your machine with monofilament thread on the top and neutral machine embroidery thread on the bottom.

2. Set the machine for straight stitching.

3. Drop the feed dogs.

4. Remove the sewing machine presser foot.

5. Put the presser foot lever in the down position.

6. Place stabilizer under your project.

7. Put a hoop on top.

8. Place the project under the machine needle.

9. Put the beads inside the hoop circle to keep them from rolling away.

Setup for machine beading

STITCHING THE BEADS

1. Pull up the thread from the bottom and take several stitches to anchor. Use 2 fingers to push the bead right up to the needle. The hole in the bead should be facing up.

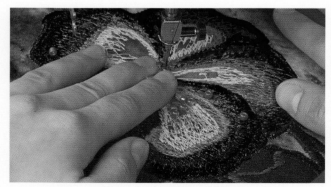

Use your fingers to set the bead in the right stitching spot.

2. With the wheel (not with the accelerator pedal), lower the needle through the bead.

3. Place your hands on the hoop and straight stitch directly into the bead 4–5 times.

4. Bring the needle up and come out of the bead the same way you went in. The bead should pop up.

The bead pops up.

5. Take several stitches to anchor the bead. I usually stitch around each bead to be sure it is anchored.

Dos and Don'ts ....

■ Do use a stiff tear-away stabilizer under your piece as you stitch.

■ Do use a sharp quilting or topstitch needle for beading.

■ Do anchor your stitching by doing some straight stitching around the bead.

■ Do consider using a hoop, like the Halo. This weighted hoop sits on top and doesn't need to be clamped.

■ Do wear eye protection, in case a bead or a needle breaks.

■ Don't start to stitch until you move your fingers out of the way. Place your hands on the hoop while stitching.

■ Don't force a needle through the hole of a bead—the bead will not stretch. Pick another bead or get a smaller needle.

....

SKILL BUILDER:
Machine Couching

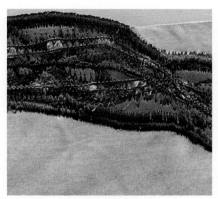

Branch detail of *Wisteria Flower Study* (page 97)

A variety of couching feet are available for different sewing machines, but the simplest method uses a straight/zigzag foot, which usually has a groove down the top center. Use that groove to guide your couching thread through the machine.

MATERIALS AND TOOLS

For more information about my recommendations, see Choosing Materials and Tools (page 17). For ordering information, see Resources (page 111).

- Monofilament thread
- Machine embroidery thread
- Straight/zigzag presser foot
- Novelty yarn
- Removable marker (I like to use blackboard chalk.)

SETTING UP

1. Put the feed dogs down. (See Setting Up the Machine, page 18.)

2. Set the stitch width for a zigzag that is wide enough to encase the yarn.

3. Set the stitch length at a moderate length (3.5mm).

4. Thread the machine with monofilament thread on top and a neutral embroidery thread on the bottom.

5. Attach the straight/zigzag foot.

STITCHING

The yarn runs through the groove and back through the hole of the presser foot.

1. Thread the yarn through the hole in the presser foot.

2. Position your project where you want the couching to start.

3. Drop the feed dogs or turn the stitch length to 0. Take several stitches to anchor the yarn.

4. Raise the feed dogs or reset the stitch length back to a moderate length.

5. Stitch across the surface of the project, guiding the yarn through the hole in the presser foot. You can maneuver the direction by holding the yarn in one hand and moving the piece with the other.

Guide the fabric with your left hand and keep tension on the couching thread with your right.

6. At the end of the line, drop the feed dogs or turn the stitch length to 0; then take several more stitches to anchor the yarn.

Dos and Don'ts ....

- Do choose yarns that are an appropriate size and material for couching. Preview each yarn on the piece first to determine if it is the right size, color, and texture for your design. Keep in mind that the yarn should enhance, rather than overwhelm, your artwork. Although I would "never say never" to any yarn choice, I avoid bulky, highly textured yarns because they would draw too much attention away from the other elements of my quilt. Of course, if I were working on a bold, bulky design, they might be just right!

- Do mark your line with a removable marker so you can see where you're going. I prefer white, green, or blue blackboard chalk because it's easy to remove.

- Don't use red or orange chalk for marking. The color can be hard to remove.

....

SKILL BUILDER:
Binding Quilts with Irregular Edges

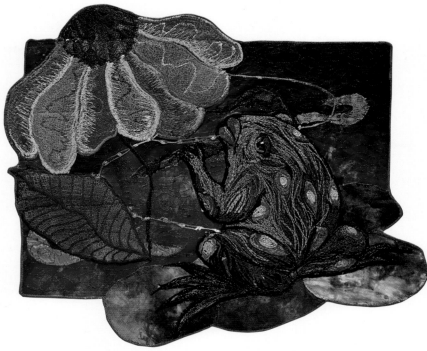

Floral Canopy, 13″ × 16″, by Ellen Anne Eddy, 2008; owned by Debby Leonard

Corded, stitched binding allows me to have a quilt in any shape I want.

MATERIALS AND TOOLS

For more information about my recommendations, see Choosing Materials and Tools (page 17). For ordering information, see Resources (page 111).

- Straight/zigzag stitching foot

- Buttonhole foot with a 2-channel escape, or zigzag (satin stitch) foot with a channel underneath

- Cotton crochet thread, size 3, in white or black

- Sewers Aid thread lubricant

- 40-weight polyester embroidery thread

Letting an image push its way past the straight lines of your quilt edge is a way to add life and a sense of movement to the design. And who says the quilt edge has to be straight?

Corded buttonhole binding is a wonderful way to bind an irregularly shaped quilt. With this technique, you stitch a length of cotton crochet thread to the quilt's edge, and then completely cover it with tightly spaced buttonhole stitching to bind the crochet thread to the quilt edge. The result is a flexible binding that will follow all the contours of your quilt.

You decide the binding color by choosing the color of embroidery thread to use for the buttonhole stitching. Contrasting thread will contain the edge, whereas thread that matches the color of the quilt edge will make your quilt expand outside its borders. Use good-quality thread for this technique. To strengthen your thread, put Sewers Aid lubricant (see Resources, page 111) on it.

1. Trim the quilt so it is exactly the size and shape you want. If it has very sharp, square corners, snip across their tips to make them slightly rounded because it is easier to achieve smooth stitches around blunt corners. Likewise, if there are very sharp, odd edges, snip across them to make them easier to cover.

Run the crochet thread through the zigzag foot.

2. Thread the machine with embroidery thread and run the cotton crochet thread through the back of the straight/zigzag foot. Set the machine for a zigzag stitch at about three-quarters of your machine's maximum width. Set the stitch length slightly longer than satin stitch.

3. Find a reasonably straight area, and line up the center of the zigzag foot with the quilt's edge. Drop the feed dogs, or turn the stitch length to 0, and take a few stitches to anchor the thread.

4. Raise the feed dogs, or reset the stitch length, and sew a zigzag stitch all around the edges of the quilt, couching the cotton crochet cord to the edge of the quilt. If the edge of the quilt ruffles, you can pull on the cord at the end of any straight segment to tighten the edge back into place.

Couch cotton crochet thread to the edge of the quilt.

5. When you have stitched all the way around the quilt, drop the feed dogs again and sew a few stitches to anchor the thread. Trim away the ends of the cotton crochet thread.

6. Put the buttonhole foot on the machine. Set the machine for a buttonhole stitch, with the needle position to the far right. Set the stitch width to your machine's maximum. Set the stitch length to the tightest satin stitch your machine will accommodate.

Note

Back of buttonhole foot with two escape channels

The buttonhole foot is perfect for this part of the process because the two escape channels on the back of the foot allow room for the thick thread ridge you will create as you sew around the quilt.

However, this foot is not so good at controlling the crochet thread as you couch it onto the quilt. The zigzag foot, with its top center channel, is better for couching.

7. Turn the quilt over. Line up the left edge of the buttonhole foot's center prong with the quilt's edge. Working on the back of the quilt, stitch all around the edge to establish a binding line. This line will not completely cover the edge.

The first row of buttonhole stitching won't completely cover the quilt edge.

8. Turn the quilt back over and stitch all around it again, working on the front edge. As you go around, make sure you have covered any bare spots. To completely cover the edge with stitching, you may need to make extra stitches at the corners.

Making another round of buttonhole stitching from the front

Note

At leaf points, stitch all the way across the end of the point, then turn and sew across that line of stitching as you stitch down the other side of the leaf.

You may occasionally need to make one more round of stitching, but usually two rounds of buttonhole stitching will cover the edge sufficiently.

SKILL BUILDING PROJECT:
In-Depth Flower Study

Water Lily, 14˝ × 11˝, by Ellen Anne Eddy, 2010

Photo by Ellen Anne Eddy

Water lily

Whenever my father went bass fishing, he would come home with more than bass because he knew I never wanted to eat the fish. He almost always brought me a white, wild water lily because he knew I loved them. I was an adult before I found out they were protected and it was illegal to pick them.

Very simple C and S shapes make up a water lily. You can use the hard-edge appliqué stitch (page 24) to create this lovely water lily study, which could fit into any pond—or quilt.

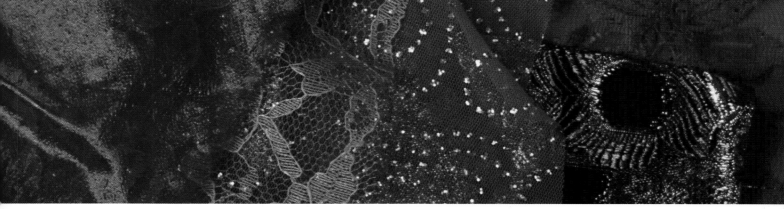

Water lily sheers

Components

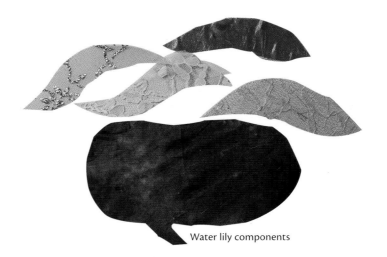

Water lily components

- **Petals:** S and C shapes

- **Center:** Smaller S shapes

- **Leaf:** Modified circle

- **Stems:** Wandering stitched lines

- **Viewpoint:** Eye level

MATERIALS AND TOOLS

For more information about my recommendations, see Choosing Materials and Tools (page 17). For ordering information, see Resources (page 111).

- Fat quarter of hand-dyed fabric for the background

- Assorted scraps of lace, organza, and lamé in white and pastels for the flower petals and in deep-water blues, greens, and purples for the leaves

- 11″ × 14″ rectangle of polyester felt

- ½ yard of nonwoven iron-on stabilizer

- 1 yard of 20″-wide repositionable fusible webbing

- Assorted metallic threads in reds, oranges, and pinks for the flowers and in greens and purples for the leaves

- 40-weight polyester embroidery thread in a neutral color for the bobbin

- Zigzag darning foot

- Size 90 topstitch needle

- Nonstick pressing cloth

- Hoop

- Tack gun (*optional*)

Metallic threads in pinks, oranges, reds, and purples embellish the water lily.

Fused Appliqué

1. Peel back a layer of paper from the repositionable fusible webbing and pat a sheer scrap onto it. It should stick nicely.

2. Cut the flower shapes from the webbing-backed sheer. I find S and C shapes work nicely for water lily petals. Cut a variety of shapes, as all petals aren't exactly the same. Cut as many as you like from each sheer scrap. I keep my shapes in plastic bags, divided by color range or shape.

3. Peel the backing paper off the water lily shapes and start to build your flower on the nonstick pressing cloth.

This water lily is based from a point along a horizontal line. The petals generate from there.

4. Fold the pressing cloth over the flower.

5. Put the tip of the iron directly into the middle of the flower, but don't iron it all. You just want to fuse the center together.

Fuse the center.

6. Let the flower cool a bit, and then peel it off the pressing cloth. The flower will stick together in the center, allowing you to keep the pieces together as you place it on the background.

7. Make a stabilizer sandwich (page 19) for the flower and another for the leaf.

Fused flower

8. Place the flower on the stabilizer sandwich and cover it with the pressing cloth. Set the iron at rayon and press the flower in place with heat and steam.

Iron on the stabilizer sandwich

SKILL BUILDER: Building Edge-to-Edge Color

For smaller flower petals, it's good to establish dimension through color. As you embroider each petal edge with different colors, some of them will fall to the back; others will come to the front. Because they're differently shaded, each will have a definite direction. Edge-to-edge color brings a flower to life.

For more about the stitches used to embellish this project, see Zigzag Stitch (pages 20 and 21).

Watch Your Angle ....

As you move the fabric under the needle, you will move seamlessly from one stitch to another. Refer to this list to help you remember which angle works best for each type of stitching.

STITCH	ANGLE
Connecting	Sideways
Fill-in	Sideways
Outline	Slanted
Shading	Slanted
Smoothing	Straight
Bulky outline	Straight
Garnet	Circular

1. Starting with the flower, use the slanted outline stitch to encase an edge.

Outline the edge.

2. Continuing to work with the fabric at a slanted angle, shade that edge well into the middle of the petal.

Shade the edge.

3. Smooth the edge by stitching straight along the side of the slanted outline stitches, connecting the shading stitches and the outline stitches. The finished edge should smoothly carry the color into the petal's interior.

Finished edge outlined, shaded, and smoothed

4. Repeat Step 1 for the other edge of the petal. I outlined in a bright red.

Outline the opposite side.

5. Swing into the petal and repeat Steps 2 and 3 to shade and smooth the other edge of the petal.

Shade and smooth the opposite side.

6. A wiggle of bright green thread in the slanted outline stitch sparks the petal to life. The width of the line changes as you turn the fabric.

The spark line

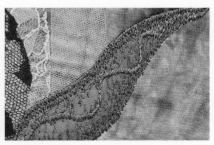

The finished petal has an inner and outer edge. The wiggle of green helps define the upward and outward energy of the flower. Edge-to-edge shading is easy, fast, and dramatic.

Stitching

EMBROIDERING THE WATER LILY AND LEAF

A wide range of colors adds to the rich texture.

1. Repeat the stitching edge-to-edge color process for the rest of the petals.

Finished water lily

2. Cut out the water lily just outside the stitching. This cuts away all the distortion, leaving a beautiful flower. Set the flower aside while you work on the leaf.

Cut out the water lily.

3. Fuse the leaf onto a stabilizer sandwich. Shade and outline the leaf. I used a purple spiral garnet stitch to shade the leaf and then outlined with dark green.

Stitching leaf detail

4. Cut out the leaf just outside the stitching.

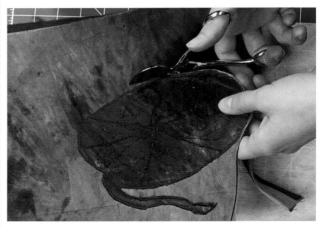

Cut out the leaf.

Embroidered water lily leaf

APPLIQUÉING THE WATER LILY AND LEAF

1. Prepare the quilt surface by applying a nonwoven stabilizer to the background fabric.

2. Use a tack gun or pins to attach the water lily and leaf to the quilt surface.

Attach the flower and leaf.

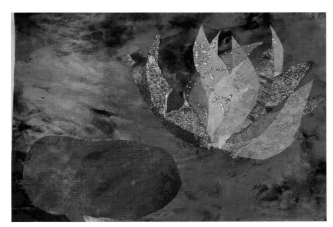

Unstitched version of *Water Lily*

3. Stitch the flower and leaf to the quilt surface, using the slanted outline stitch in colors that match the outlining threads. (To learn more about appliqué, see Free-Motion Appliqué, page 24.) Make the stitch width just wide enough to cover the edges completely.

Stitch down the flower.

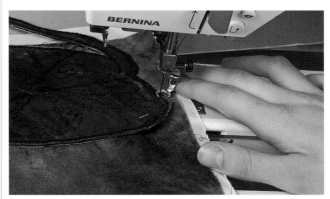

Stitch down the leaf.

4. Create a stem with the bulky outline stitch.

5. Use the slanted outline stitch to create a sepal at the flower's center. To make the sepal narrower at both ends, sweep the fabric to an angle as you sew.

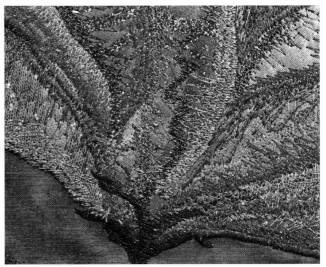

Finished water lily flower detail

SKILL BUILDING PROJECT:
Creating Abstract Design and a Visual Path

Jazzed: Spring Fling, 11″ × 14″, by Ellen Anne Eddy, 2010

For the background fabric, I chose a dark, mottled green that makes a great universal background.

How do you do abstract design? There are several easy ways. In my Jazzed series of quilts, I reduced the flowers to simple shapes, let the color go wild, and built a visual path across the surface of each quilt to carry the eye through the design. The result is that the rhythm of the piece is its strongest design element. All of these approaches create fabulous abstract work.

For this project, I took some of my favorite early spring flowers—tulips, forsythia, cherry blossoms, and squill—and let them dance across the quilt surface.

MATERIALS AND TOOLS

For more information about my recommendations, see Choosing Materials and Tools (page 17). For ordering information, see Resources (page 111).

- ½ yard of hand-dyed fabric for the background

- Scraps of yellow, peach, pink, and green hand-dyed fabric for the flowers

- Double-sided fusible webbing

- 11″ × 14″ rectangle of polyester felt

- ½ yard of nonwoven iron-on stabilizer

- 1 yard of 20″-wide repositionable fusible webbing

- Assorted threads

- 40-weight polyester embroidery thread in a neutral color for the bobbin

- Zigzag darning foot

- Size 90 topstitch needle

- Nonstick pressing cloth

- Hoop

- Tack gun (*optional*)

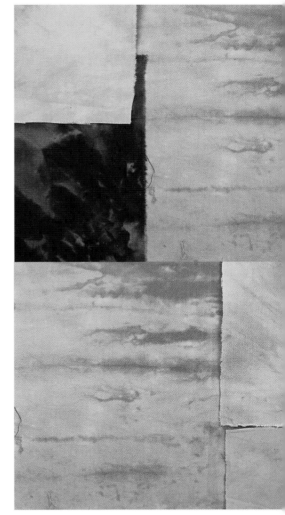

The flower fabrics are light, luminous hand-dyed fabrics that glow against the green. They're variegated, just like real flower petals.

Cutting Shapes

TULIP

Components

- **Petals:** Teardrop shapes
- **Leaves:** Broadsword shapes

CHERRY BLOSSOM

This cherry blossom is from the weeping cherry in my front yard.

Components

- **Blossoms:** Teardrop shapes

FORSYTHIA

The forsythia is another flower that rockets through the first garden rush. Mine blooms right next to the weeping cherry.

Components

- **Petals:** 4 (or fewer) loop shapes joined at the center

SQUILL

Squill is a tiny flower with rice-shaped petals that form a cup-shaped bloom.

Squill is so delicate that I chose to make the flower entirely out of stitching.

SKILL BUILDER:
Creating a Visual Path

The visual path is a design concept. Creating a pathway across the art's surface brings it to life and gives it a sense of motion. There are several easy ways to create a visual path; several are used in this project.

1. Place the tulip on the quilt's background fabric. This S-shaped flower already puts the design into motion by leading the viewer visually across the quilt's surface.

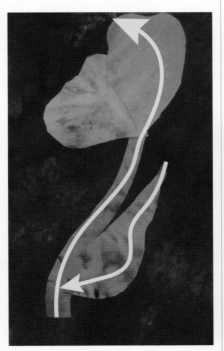

The major design element

2. Build a path around the design element. The cherry blossoms are little stepping-stones that help the eye travel across the surface.

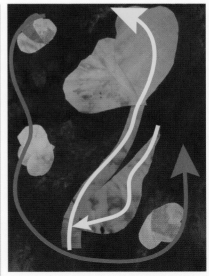

Smaller elements create a pathway around the element.

3. Support the path with smaller elements. Small sprigs of squill dance between the spaces. The forsythia blooms fill in the space and continue to support the path.

Forsythia blooms and squill fill in the space between.

SKILL BUILDER:
Progressive Shading

Progressive shading carries waves of color across the surface. Start shading with the darkest threads, adding one color layer after another. Each line of color will fill in a little more space and will stretch the color further. There's the outline, the shading out from the side of the outline, and then the smoothing row that joins them.

For more about the zigzag stitches used to create the embellishment, see Zigzag Stitch (pages 20 and 21).

Watch Your Angle ....

As you move the fabric under the needle, you will move seamlessly from one stitch to another. Refer to this list to help you remember which angle works best for each type of stitching.

STITCH	ANGLE
Connecting	Sideways
Fill-in	Sideways
Outline	Slanted
Shading	Slanted
Smoothing	Straight
Bulky outline	Straight
Garnet	Circular

Stitching

To learn the stitching techniques used in this project, see Stitch Essentials (pages 18–24).

Stabilizing Larger Flowers ....

Plump, full flowers are a delight to embellish, but distortion is always a problem. Any time you completely shade in a space that is more than 3″ in dimension, you can bank on a certain amount of ruffling.

To avoid distortion, stitch the tulips and cherry blossoms on a stabilizer sandwich (page 19) and then cut away the rippled edges. The result is flat and lovely embroidery, which can be applied directly to the quilt's background fabric with a slanted free-motion zigzag stitch (see Free-Motion Appliqué, page 24). The flower will look as if it's always been there, but the distortion will be lying on the studio floor.

BUILDING BEAUTIFUL COLOR

Building color with thread is a bit like mixing paint color, but with one major difference. When you mix paint, all the colors blend with each other, disappearing into a new color. There's a real danger of coming out with mud. When you're mixing with thread, however, the colors stay themselves, all stitched in layers. The eye itself mixes the color. Almost impossible color combinations mix together clearly and beautifully. I usually stitch from dark to light. Small bits of all the colors will show, but the last color is the one you will see the most.

THREAD CHOICES

Choose a wide range of colors in the shade you want, going much lighter and darker than the effect you want. Then add a shocker and a shader thread (see Shockers and Shaders, pages 15 and 16) to spark and shade the piece. For my mostly red tulip, I used purple threads as the shocker and shader colors.

Tulip threads

Tulip

1. Start by outlining and shading with the darkest thread.

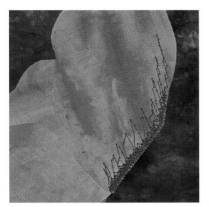

First line of stitching in dark red

2. Fill in with the slanted shading stitch in a slightly lighter thread.

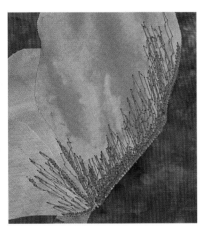

Lighter red stitching

3. Stitch 2 rows of the slanted shading stitch, using the shocker and shader threads to create the ridge down the tulip's center, as well as to shade the flower base.

Purple shading

The two layers of shading weight the bottom of the flower with their darker tones.

4. Add red-orange shading in the midrange to establish the basic flower color.

Red-orange stitching establishes the basic color.

5. Continue shading in the brighter orange thread to continue the tone.

Brighter orange stitching continues the tone.

6. Add more shading in another shocker color. I used orange-pink, which is so out of place that it jars the eye. However, blended with the other colors, it keeps the tone lively and exciting.

Bright orange-pink shading acts as a shocker.

7. The very hot pink edge pops the top of the tulip. Use it to sew a row of the slanted outline stitch around the edge of the flower. (You will add more hot pink later.)

Bright hot-pink edging

FINISHING THE TULIP AND LEAF

This range of greens gives three different tones and colors.

1. Using the slanted outline stitch, create veins and folds in the leaves. Use contrasting threads to add dimension to the leaves.

Leaf detailing

2. Outline the leaves in the same greens you used for the veins and folds.

3. Use the slanted outline stitch to create a stem.

Stitch down the stem.

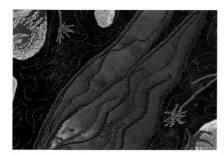

The finished leaf

4. Cut the flower and leaves out of the stabilizer sandwich.

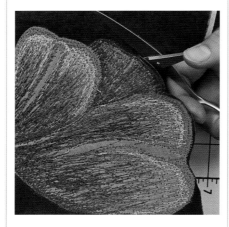

5. Tack the flower and leaf units in place on the quilt's background fabric.

6. Use the slanted outline stitch to appliqué the flower and leaves in place, using the same thread colors you used to outline the flower.

Cherry Blossoms

Cherry blossom threads

I chose a wide range of pinks, with a purple shader, for the cherry blossoms. Choosing different color combinations builds a rich color range and echoes the kind of dappled light seen in a garden.

Because these are smaller flowers, they don't require as much shading. But if you shade each side of the petal, you can build up a lovely texture.

1. Stitch a row with the slanted outline stitch and another row with the shading stitch, using the same thread for both rows. This gives each petal a shaded outline with a spiral finish.

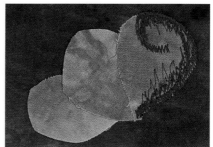

Outline shading with a spiral detail

2. Follow the spiral with the sideways fill-in stitch and the slanted outline stitch in a contrasting thread color. The other edge of the flower wraps around the spiral and fills in with the shade.

3. Repeat Steps 1 and 2 for the other petals, using different threads for each petal.

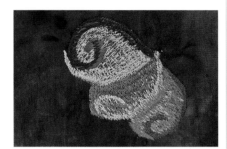

Finished cherry blossom

4. Cut out the cherry blossoms and tack them to the quilt background.

5. Appliqué the blossoms to the quilt with the same color used for the edge with the spiral detail.

Apply the flower.

6. Use green thread and an outline stitch to add the sepal.

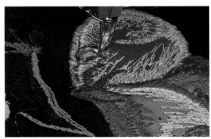

Add the sepal.

Forsythia

These bright yellows make a great blend for forsythia. The periwinkle is a fabulous complementary shade for veining.

The forsythias are stitched minimally and can be stitched directly onto the quilt background. Keep a stabilizer sheet under the quilt background fabric as you stitch.

1. Working directly on the quilt's background, stitch a slanted outline just wide enough to cover the edges of the petals. Start and end with a curve at the top of the petals.

The curves at the end of the petals round out the blooms.

2. Fill in the opposite side of the petal by outlining in a different yellow.

Finish the outline in a different yellow.

3. Straight stitch the veins in periwinkle.

Veining forsythia

Although the forsythias are small, the thread colors keep the effect rich and textural.

Squill

The eye-popping colors of the squill work well because the stitched flowers are just tiny bits of thread.

1. Working directly on the quilt background, stitch arced stems in a narrow free-motion zigzag to create the stems and leaves.

Squill leaves and stems are tucked in between the forsythia and cherry blossoms.

2. Stitch a zigzag star in bright blue thread for the squill flowers. To make the star, work around a circle point, stitching short rows out to the side and back to the center. To change the width of the stitching, change the stitching angle.

Stitch the squill.

The very bright green and blue threads make the squill pop.

Stippling

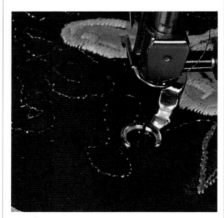

Stippling

Fill in the empty spaces on the quilt background with a free-motion straight stitch in a stipple pattern. For the stippling, I chose a multicolored green metallic thread that sparks the surface. My favorite thread for stippling is sliver thread, a shiny flat thread that comes in many colors and can be used in the bobbin. See Resources (page 111).

I often sign my quilts in the stippling while doing bobbin work, so I've learned to do it backward. For more on bobbin work, see A Case for Working on the Back of the Fabric (page 24).

Signature in stippling

Finishing the Quilt

After the quilt is stippled, it's ready to be backed, quilted, and bound. I use a needle-punched cotton batting and a pretty hand-dyed fabric for the backing. I quilt minimally around the design elements with a straight stitch and monofilament thread. Then I add a corded buttonhole binding around the edge (see Binding Quilts with Irregular Edges, page 30).

Planning Flowers from Simple Shapes

Your strongest skill as an artist is often the ability to simplify things. If you start by simplifying your flowers' shapes, you are free to work without patterns and without fussiness. Make flowers not from how they actually are shaped but from how they appear to be shaped. That sounds like cheating, but it's not. It allows you to easily shape your flowers and to make them abstract if you wish.

Simple circles can be used to make numerous kinds of flowers. Other flowers are formed from cup-and-saucer shapes, bell shapes, or heart shapes. You can ornament any of these shapes with stitched petals, stamens, edges, and leaves.

Each flower study on the following pages shows a photo of the flower in nature, an unstitched version of the flower elements in place on the background fabric, and a stitched version of the flower in appliqué and machine embroidery, including details of the flower and leaf. You can use these shapes and thread embellishment ideas when you design your own flowers.

Although the stitching ignites the flowers, the raw shapes themselves are so exciting that it's worth looking at them as well. That's why I've provided a photo of the unstitched version of each flower study. For a different look, you could easily stitch the floral elements with invisible thread instead of ornamenting them with machine embroidery. It's a design choice.

Detail of *Jazzed: Garden Heart* (page 70)
Simple shapes make an arresting statement.

FLOWER STUDIES:
Circles and Balls of Blossoms

The elements in fantasy flowers are similar to the elements in real flowers. The differences are mostly color choices and less-regular shapes.

Many blooms are really a ball of blossoms or petals. Hydrangea, phlox, roses, lilacs, and so many others can be made from a simple circle or cone shape that is then detailed with thread petals. This approach works best for flowers that have an uncountable number of petals or that are being viewed from a distance. These flowers start as circles—some smooth and some more oval or wobbly.

Jazzed: Encircled, 11″ × 14″, by Ellen Anne Eddy, 2010

I started with a visual path of green circles. Then I made two flowers from off-center circles and surrounded them with smaller satellites. The stitching echoes the flower shapes. Small lines of straight stitching, with garnet circles like beads, fill in the space.

Circles and Balls of Blossoms: Grape Hyacinth

These tiny spring offerings grow in the lawn as well as in garden beds. They seem to dance under the daffodil blooms.

In the language of flowers, hyacinth acknowledges sorrow and a need for forgiveness.

Grape hyacinths are so small that it is hard to see their circle flowers without close-up photography.

Photo by Ellen Anne Eddy

COMPONENTS

- **Flower:** Circles of varying sizes
- **Leaves and stems:** Gently curved sword shapes

COMPOSITION

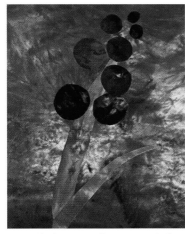

Unstitched version of *Grape Hyacinth Flower Study*—Graded circles go up the stem. The view starts from eye level at the bottom of the flower and goes to above eye level at the top of the flower.

COLOR TALK

The balls are plumped with a darker rim of color, followed by a lighter inner shade, all set off with a ruffled center in white iridescent thread.

Gentle, wiggly zigzag lines in different greens define the stems.

Circles and Balls of Blossoms: *Zinnia*

Zinnias might be my favorite annuals. My dad grew these for me, too. I still love their brilliant pink, red, and orange displays. They're hot-weather flowers that survive dry heat or the dog days of summer.

Photo by Ellen Anne Eddy

COMPONENTS

- **Flower:** Oval base
- **Stems:** Stiff, straight
- **Leaves:** Elongated loops

COMPOSITION

Unstitched version of *Zinnia Flower Study*—The flower base sits on top of the stem, but the leaves on zinnias point down rather than up. Curved narrow tops fit the stem.

STITCHING SENSE

The petals spread out at the edge. I chose an inner center on the flower base and began to rotate the stitching around it. Small, yellow, straight-stitched stamens pop out of the center. Both warm and cool pinks balance out the color temperature.

The leaves are simple loops veined with zigzag stitching that is worked out to the side to create that delicate line.

Circles and Balls of Blossoms: Marigold

Marigolds love hot weather. My father used to grow man-in-the-moon marigolds that came up to my knees. I now grow pots of them, so that I have enough for my salad, too. In the language of flowers, they are a golden gift.

COMPONENTS

- **Bloom:** Oval
- **Petals:** Too many to cut or count; stitching will define
- **Leaves:** Thick sword shapes
- **Sepal:** Rough triangle
- **Viewpoint:** Side view

COMPOSITION

Unstitched version of *Marigold Flower Study*—These components could be almost any flower with many petals.

STITCHING SENSE

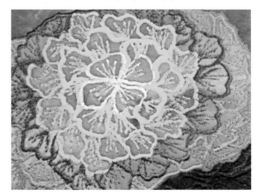

Ruffled stitching coming out from the center really defines this as a marigold. The row of purple stitching builds dimension.

It was easier to do the spiky leaf points in stitching. Each leaf has two shades of green, separated by the leaf vein to make the leaves seem twofold.

Butterfly and Allium, 14″x 18″
by Ellen Anne Eddy, 2010

This allium is made with a simple purple circle that is stitched with star shapes and appliquéd with stitched points.

Marigold and Ladybug, 10″ × 13″
by Ellen Anne Eddy, 2010

A single oval of hand-painted organza stitched with yellow and purple threads makes up this marigold.

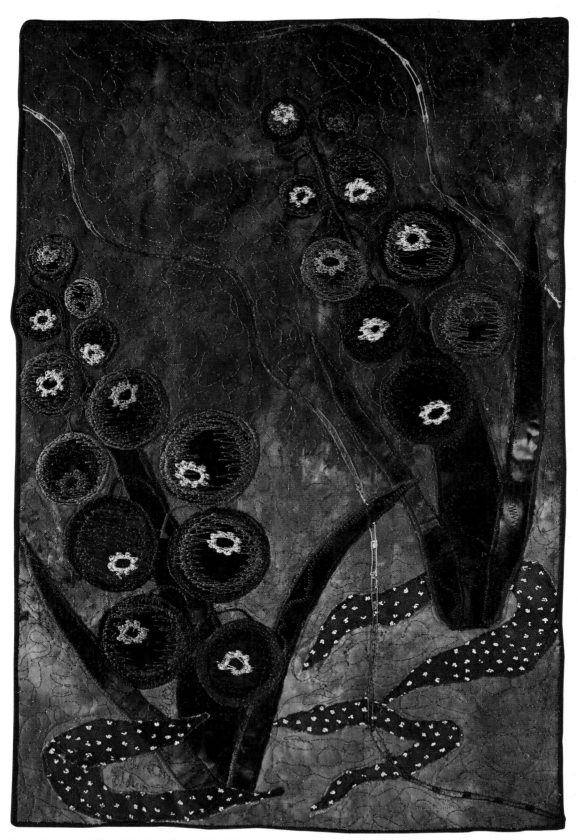

Spring Hyacinths, 20″ × 13″, by Ellen Anne Eddy, 2010

These blue globes glow against the red-violet sky. Small C shapes of rhinestone organza suggest spring puddles around the blooms.

FLOWER STUDIES: Hearts

Some flowers and many leaves are heart-shaped. Because this is a shape that is connected to all kinds of symbolism, it has a wider range of expression than other shapes. You can leave your heart, lose your heart, break your heart, give your heart—and find it in the candy aisle on Valentine's Day.

Hearts on the Vine, 11″ × 14″, by Ellen Anne Eddy, 2010

Decorated as candy hearts, the heart shapes are both flowers and candy, offerings of our daydream loves. I placed some organza and commercial lace hearts on the side to shadow the heart blossoms.

Hearts:
Bleeding Heart and Dutchman's Breeches

These wonderful spring shrubs bloom in early April in the darkest shade of the garden. Dutchman's breeches are white, and bleeding hearts are pink. They are bright spots in a spring garden. In the language of flowers, bleeding hearts symbolize undying love.

Photo by Ellen Anne Eddy

COMPONENTS

- **Petals:** Many heart shapes with 2 dangles
- **Stems:** Curved
- **Leaves:** Lobed, ragged

COLOR TALK

Loose zigzag stitching texturizes the leaves. The fill-in stitching is done at a 40° to 60° angle, like an outline stitch but moving your hands much faster. It creates a raggedy zigzag-stitched leaf.

A line of purple metallic thread attaches each heart to the vine and helps to define its plump, rounded shape.

COMPOSITION

Unstitched version of *Bleeding Heart Flower Study*—Here's a sprig of both Dutchman's breeches and bleeding heart. Both vines dangle heart shapes under ragged lobed leaves.

Planning Flowers from Simple Shapes 55

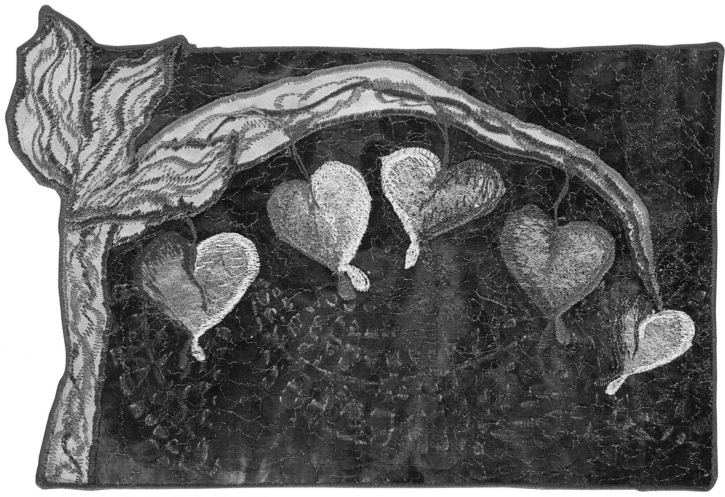

Hearts on the Line, 11″ × 9″, by Ellen Anne Eddy, 2010

These flowers grow in the deep shade, so it was fun to quilt them in background fabric that evokes shade. The color range moves from light pink to plum purple. Purple oil-stick leaf rubbings help fill in the background.

FLOWER STUDIES: Bells

There are so many bell-shaped flowers in a garden—hostas, blue bells, cathedral bells, Japanese lanterns, bellflowers, trumpet vines, and morning glories. I also like to hang actual bells in my garden to give the wind a voice.

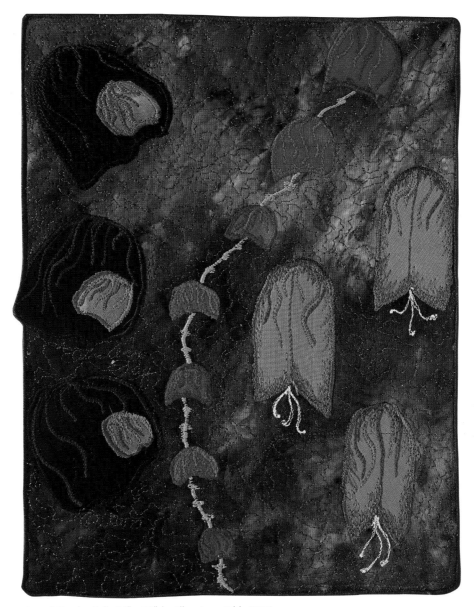

Jazzed: Garden Bells, 14″ × 10″, by Ellen Anne Eddy, 2010

Many Japanese gardens have rainspouts of water-chime bells on a chain. These bells of differing sizes remind me of that. But these are flowers, ringing their silent bells in the breeze. Light green accents create the stamens in the large bells, as well as the vine between the smaller ones.

Bells: *Hosta*

Although hostas are grown more often for their leaves than their flowers, I love their flowers. Hosta blooms start as delicate bud bells and expand into bell-shaped flowers.

I was underwhelmed when I found out that my new house had mostly hostas in the front yard. That was before I knew how tough and showy they are. Now I tend to mulch with hostas.

Photo by Ellen Anne Eddy

COMPONENTS

- **Flowers:** Small bell shapes
- **Leaves:** Many large heart or shield shapes
- **Stem:** One, long

COMPOSITION

Unstitched version of *Hosta Flower Study*—Hosta flowers float off a single stem above a mass of green leaves.

STITCHING SENSE

These flowers were embroidered on a separate stabilizer sandwich, with bell shapes cut from Angelina fiber and commercial lace.

Light green stitching details the outer shapes of the leaves. Many hosta leaves have amazing patterns in dark and bright green.

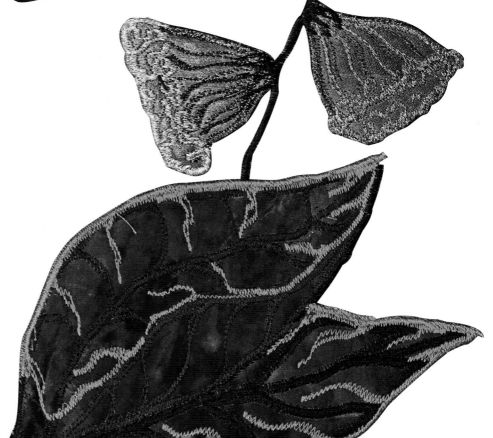

Bells: $\mathscr{Salvia}$

Although salvia comes in purple and white, red is its most dramatic color. A distant relative to herbal sage, it is really an ornamental annual. Tall and demanding in a pot, it's a great garden accent.

Photo by Ellen Anne Eddy

COMPONENTS

- **Flowers:** Bell shapes that stand straight out from the stalk opposite each other
- **Leaves:** Toothed shield shapes
- **Stem:** Straight stalk

COMPOSITION

Unstitched version of *Salvia Flower Study*—Salvia have bells of blossoms that dangle from the stalk.

COLOR TALK

Light yellow-green and dark purple stitching offers highlights and shadows for these mostly red blooms.

Salvia's pale ruffled rim around the leaf is easily echoed in zigzag stitching.

Bells: Japanese Lanterns

These lovely orange bell shapes are actually fruit, blooming from late summer to fall. The Victorians brought them back from Japan. The orange fruit has a papery texture, and they dry beautifully, like little bells under leafy foliage.

Photo by Ellen Anne Eddy

COMPONENTS

- **Flowers:** Several bell shapes
- **Leaves:** Spatulate (wider at the tip than at the stem) with points
- **Stem:** Gently curved or straight

COMPOSITION

Unstitched version of *Japanese Lantern Flower Study*—Three lanterns float under the leaves of this Japanese lantern plant.

COLOR TALK

Several shades of orange and red-orange make these blossoms glow. The bright green stems make the flowers pop.

The leaves make a green canopy over the blooms.

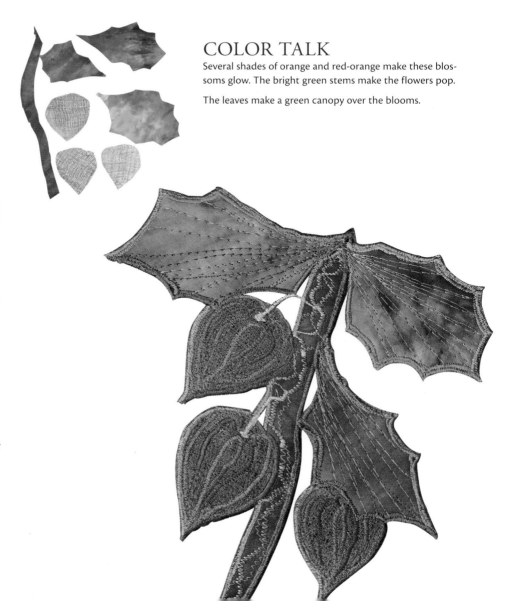

Bells: *Cathedral Bells*

Pat Winter, a master crazy quilter and gardener, gave me cathedral bells for my garden. Almost a wildflower, they bloom from late July to early fall. In the language of flowers, they represent everlasting love.

Photo by Ellen Anne Eddy

COMPONENTS

- **Blooms:** Bell shapes growing in cascades down one side of the flower

- **Leaves:** Jagged shield shapes

COMPOSITION

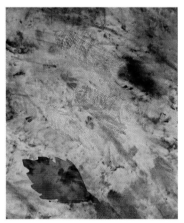

Unstitched version of *Cathedral Bells Flower Study*—Pink cheesecloth creates a delicate texture for these bellflowers.

COLOR TALK

The flowers are rimmed in soft pink with a pale yellow ridge. Sepals and stems are created from threadwork.

Straight rows of zigzag stitching from the bottom of the leaf create veins in varied greens.

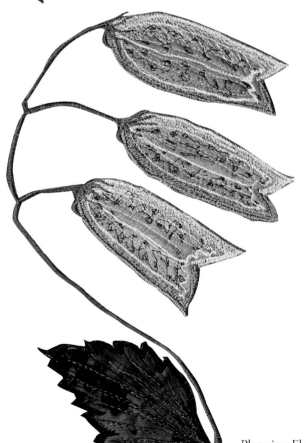

Lady Mantis 2, 26″ × 16″, by Ellen Anne Eddy, 2007

This lovely lady is cavorting in the hostas by moonlight. The moon, made from Angelina and Crystalina fibers and trapped thread (see Using Angelina Fiber, page 25), echoes the playful white flowers that float around her.

Morning Glories, 20″ × 20″, by Ellen Anne Eddy, 2010

It's hard to know which is more glorious: the dragonflies, the morning sunshine in the hand-dyed fabric, or the flowers. These morning glories are viewed from beneath their bell-shaped rims. The star shape suggests their rigid bell structure.

Balcony Scene, 30″ × 36″, by Ellen Anne Eddy, 2003

A simple bell shape with a cup cut from cheesecloth creates this calla lily. Bright stitching illuminates the rim of the lily, while darker rows shade the bottom cup.

SKILL BUILDER:
Fantasy Flowers

Fantasy flowers can be anything your heart desires. Almost all of these flowers are simple geometric shapes. They are drawn as circles, stars, triangles, and teardrops, and then divided in different ways. Though they are not found in nature, their structure is perfectly natural and representative of many flowers. *Butterfly Garden* is rich with examples of fantasy flowers with simple shapes.

The design of these flowers must follow some very basic rules to make them work visually. To make them recognizable, you need to create the visual clues that say "these are flowers."

Butterfly Garden, 27″ × 59″, by Ellen Anne Eddy, 2010

CIRCLES

Circles make all kinds of amazing flowers. So many flowers can be viewed as balls, cups, or saucers. Many are a combination of those circular shapes.

Of course, the closer you look, the less perfect and less basic the details appear. Nature is perfect in her choices but not always in her forms. Often it's the irregularities and imperfections that make a flower most beautiful.

Saucer-shaped flower from *Butterfly Garden*—The circle is by far the most common floral shape. It is so basic that it is almost always a child's first drawn flower: a circle on a straight line.

This flower design is much more exciting for being off-center. The directional spirals put it into motion.

CUPS

Many flowers are cup shapes. Their petals bend up to reveal a chalice with the center and stamens in the bottom, like a small treasure.

Cup-shaped flower from *Butterfly Garden*—The extreme range in the petal colors and the wide width of the circle's arc confirm the bloom's cup shape. The luscious pink-purple and orange center invites us, like a bee, to come inside.

This cup-shaped flower is a simple circle divided geometrically. Each division becomes one of the petals.

SAUCERS

Many flowers radiate petals out flat from the center. These are saucer flowers. Some have a small upturned rim at the edge, while others do not.

Rimmed saucer flower from *Butterfly Garden*—The orange rim echoes the center as if it were a turned-up rim. The lime ruffled-edge stitch clarifies the petals' edges.

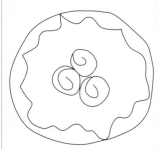

The smaller outer rim on this flower makes it a saucer. The center spirals give the feeling of seedpods.

Flowers that radiate from a center can be approached as a circle or a semi-circle, especially if you are looking at them from above. These flowers are simple but very effective because the circle gives a color center while the stitching defines the petals.

Saucer flower from *Butterfly Garden*—The complementary stripe of orange stitching pops one side of each stitched petal, putting the petals into appropriate spatial dimension.

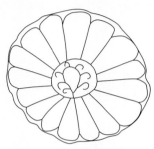

Saucer flower drawing—The petals are stitched with strong colors that separate them clearly. A small rim pops the edge visually and contains the edge.

STARS

Star flower from *Butterfly Garden*—This star flower has a strong triangular center and a golden rim. The bright gold against the soft blue pops the ridge. The star shape creates a ruffled petal edge.

Star-shaped flower drawing—The outer ridge creates the saucer rim that makes this into a floral shape.

TEARDROPS

A teardrop shape in the center of a flower gives the sense of a cup-shaped flower as seen from above.

Circle with teardrop center from *Butterfly Garden*—The purple rim maintains the flower's circle shape, while also defining the spatula-shaped green petals.

Drawing of a circle flower with a teardrop center—Scalloped detailing around the edge of the center gives the illusion of stamens.

Teardrops make an elegant petal shape or an interesting bell-shaped flower. The viewpoint for both is from an angle beneath the flower so that you can see inside.

This flower is designed to be off-center and to dangle at the end of a branch.

TRIANGLES

Triangular flower from *Butterfly Garden*—The petals are shaded from light pink to dark purple. The red-orange squiggle gives them a shimmer of light over the surface.

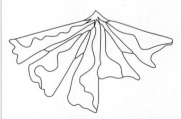

Triangular flower drawing—These triangular petals radiate out from the stamen in a fan shape, creating a great side view of the flower.

The Language of Flowers..
Victorians used flowers as an amazing code. Even today, the flowers we use often have meanings. I've included that information when I could find it because I think it's nice to know what you're saying with flowers.
....

Fantasy Flowers:
Lollipop

These are the lollipop flowers straight from child-hood. Who knew we were that smart? Who could resist them?

COMPONENTS

- **Flowers, center, and rim:** Simple circles
- **Leaves:** Slightly bent sword shapes

COMPOSITION

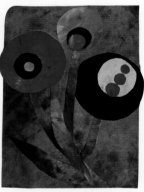

Unstitched version of *Lollipop Flower Study*—Bright hand-dyed fabric pops this bouquet so that it blooms in an arc around the center.

COLOR TALK

This is the simplest outline treatment for these fantasy leaves. Three shades of green separate the leaves. Bright orange and periwinkle threads spark this dark purple flower.

Fantasy Flowers:
Wobbly Circles

What happens if you cut your circles with irregular edges? Your fantasy flowers will become much more lifelike.

COMPONENTS

- **Flowers:** Circles with wobbly edges for the outer shape and the center

- **Leaves:** Straight sword shapes

STITCHING SENSE

The stitching echoes the same wobbly lines as the flower's edges. Garnet stitching (stitching in circles) creates the flower center. The leaf stitching creates a scalloped edge that's wild and fun.

COMPOSITION

Unstitched version of *Wobbly Circle Flower Study*—These three blooms pop straight up from the center of the flower.

Planning Flowers from Elements

Perspective, Shape, and Details

If you are going to build flowers from their elemental shapes, you need to know several pieces of information about each flower. You need to know the perspective, or from what eye level you are viewing it. You need to know the shape of the petals, the leaves, the center, and the stems. And you need to know the number of petals.

I have put all of this information together for each flower study, separating the flowers according to the different petal shapes. You can use these flower studies as you cut your own flower components, place them, and stitch them into life.

The stitching is where I live. I love what happens when I add that decorative element. But you can use these same simple shapes, without embroidery, for a quick and easy abstract effect. I have included a photo of the unstitched version of each flower to give you an idea of how the abstract design would look.

Jazzed: Garden Heart, 11″ × 14″, by Ellen Anne Eddy, 2010

FLOWER STUDIES: Loop Petals

Flowers made from loop petals are almost endless—daisies, cosmos, asters, coneflowers, and black-eyed Susans are just a few.

Jazzed: Daisied, 11″ × 14″, by Ellen Anne Eddy, 2010

Daisy loops make delicious little blooms that dance across this quilt. I discovered the secret to peacock-tail coloring: It's a range of blues, purples, and teals with gold-green highlights. The combination is electric, on or off a peacock.

Loop Petals: Cosmos

Spanish priests grew cosmos in their mission gardens in Mexico. The evenly placed petals led them to christen the flower "Cosmos," the Greek word for harmony. They were always part of my father's flower garden and are always part of mine.

Photo by Ellen Anne Eddy

COMPONENTS

- **Center:** Oval
- **Petals:** Many; loop shapes
- **Stem:** Narrow, curving
- **Leaves:** Tiny fronds

COMPOSITION

Unstitched version of *Cosmos Flower Study*—The leaves and stems on a cosmos are delicate, so I stitched them in. The composition is a flower viewed from the side, which makes the center appear more oval shaped. Hand-dyed cotton in several purple shades displays highlights and shadows.

COLOR TALK

Highlights of bright pink and yellow electrify this purple and pink bloom.

To make the stems, I stitched a narrow zigzag line at an almost straight angle. I stitched the leaves at a 40° to 60° angle to create the pointy ends.

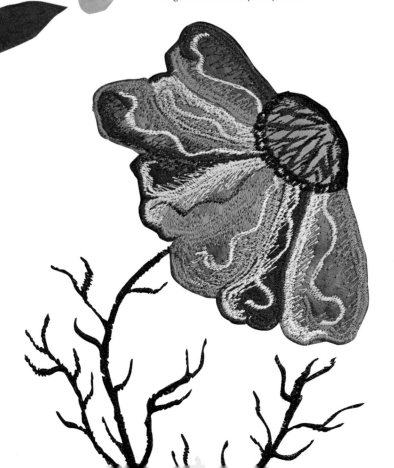

Loop Petals: *Daisy*

Daisies are the flower of childhood. We made daisy chains, we foretold our first loves, and we wore them in our hair. In the language of flowers, they represent innocence.

Photo by Ellen Anne Eddy

COMPONENTS

- **Flower:** Saucer shaped; radiating from a small, flat center
- **Petals:** Many; loop shapes
- **Leaves:** Ragged branch shapes
- **Stem:** Straight or gently curved
- **Center:** Circle shape for a top view

COMPOSITION

Unstitched version of *Daisy Flower Study*—Daisies float above their foliage on fairly long stems. Both of these show a side view with leaves arranged for two stitched stems.

COLOR TALK

White is a hard color to use alone. If you make something completely white, it has no dimension. All kinds of lace, organza, and Angelina fiber give the petals variety. Threads in blues, yellows, lavenders, and white shade the flowers. Brown and purple threads in garnet stitching texturize the center.

The leaves are ragged and branchy, stitched in three shades of green for variety.

Planning Flowers from Elements   73

Raining Daisies, 10″ × 17″, by Ellen Anne Eddy, 2010; owned by Elizabeth McGrail

Daisies rain down through the moonlit sky. Sheers, commercial lace, and Angelina fiber make luminous petals encased in pastel blue, silver, and white metallic stitching. White flowers are always difficult to shade; you need to have some variance to make them dimensional. Here I used differing metallic silvers, iridescent thread, and pastels to create shadows and highlights. Quiet purples offer an elegant color range. This range between white and purple makes a monochromatic, softly shaded daisy.

Wacky Rudabeckia, 11″ × 17″, by Ellen Anne Eddy, 2010

The black-eyed Susan (rudabeckia) is almost a wildflower. I cut large wiggly petals and leaves from cheesecloth and then shaded them with purple, brown, and green squiggly lines to add to the flower's rough edges. The striped element in the center extends the feeling of a flower grown in the wild.

Planning Flowers from Elements　75

Hunter's Moon 2, 22″ × 57″, by Ellen Anne Eddy, 2006; owned by Laura Zaranski

I love things that fly at night. Magnolia petals hang softly off the branches, as bats, owl, and moths soar through the same sky. Metallic iridescent and silver stitching softens the white blossoms and keeps these petals from being too bright.

Blossoms in the Moonlight, 15″ × 18″, by Ellen Anne Eddy, 2010

Bunnies are a big part of a garden patrolled by greyhounds. My dogs never hurt the rabbits, but they pay a lot of attention. So occasionally I do a bunny quilt. We called the bunny Blossom. Small round loops make up the blossoms on this vine. The sheers and lamé in the blossoms reflect the metallic thread. The sepal and leaves are stitched with polyester thread to separate them visually from the petals.

FLOWER STUDIES: Rice-Shaped Petals

These blooms and their leaves are simple rice shapes joined at one end. The larger leaves are joined vertically, and the smaller ones come together on a delicate vine. They burst across the quilt surface in rhythmic patterns.

Jazzed: Rice Petal Flowers, 11″ × 14″, by Ellen Anne Eddy, 2010

Most buds can be shaped as rice petals, but snowdrops, squill, spirea, and many other small spring petals are that shape as well. Many fantasy flowers can be made from the rice shape. Wild stripes of bright colors wriggle through the petal surfaces, making these fantasy flowers irresistible.

Rice-Shaped Petals: *Snowdrops*

I'd love these sweet, simple flowers even if they weren't the first things that bloom in my garden. But they are the first, and I love them all the more for it.

There's a legend that snowdrops sprang out of the earth from Eve's first tears when she left the garden. They symbolize purity and hope.

Photo by Ellen Anne Eddy

COMPONENTS

- **Petals:** Rice shapes
- **Sepal:** Small oval
- **Leaves:** Sword shapes
- **Stem:** Curve from which the petal dangles
- **Viewpoint:** From the side

COLOR TALK

Soft colors add dimensionality to white. Softly grayed, hand-dyed cotton makes the petals, and white, silver, and pale lime metallic threads make the color range zing, all without losing the sense of a white petal.

The sword-shaped leaves don't have a lot of detailing, but a squiggling line of stitching with polyester embroidery thread makes them green and growing.

COMPOSITION

Unstitched version of *Snowdrop Flower Study*—This flower has both a bud and a fully open snowdrop.

FLOWER STUDIES: C-Shaped Petals

Stalklike flowers, such as birds of paradise and daylilies, use C shapes, as do upturned saucer flowers like clematis and water lilies. For more about water lilies, see In-Depth Flower Study (pages 32–37).

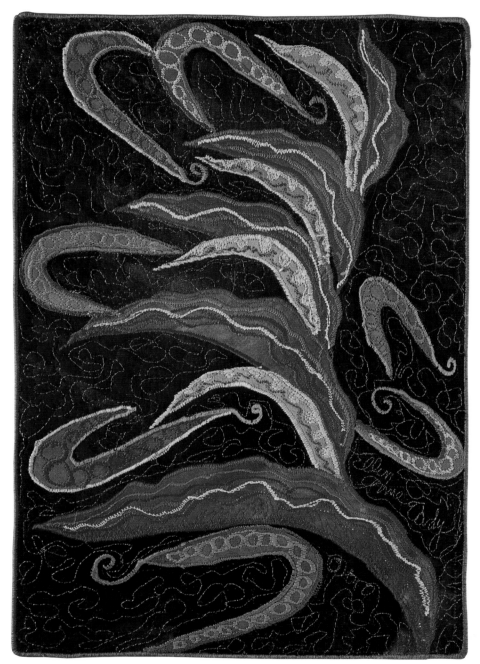

Jazzed: "C" Stalk, 11" × 14", by Ellen Anne Eddy, 2010

As I started to fit these C shapes together, they almost immediately formed into a stalk, something like ragweed or a cornstalk. The C-shaped green swirls redirect the energy back into the piece. Garnet stitching creates the wonderful circle texture on both the leaves and the green swirls.

C-Shaped Petals: Daylily

My father brought a daylily to our yard as part of his dowry when he married my mother. I took some of those lilies with me when I left home, but I lost them in a move. When I bought my current house, a friend brought me a chunk of my father's daylily from her garden. By my reckoning, this flower has been with the Eddys for almost 100 years.

Daylilies are a floral salute in the middle of a hot July. In the language of flowers, they represent coquetry.

Photo by Ellen Anne Eddy

COMPONENTS

- **Petals:** Many C shapes
- **Leaves:** Sword shapes
- **Stem:** Stiff and straight or gently curved
- **Sepal:** Triangle

COMPOSITION

Unstitched version of *Daylily Flower Study*— This lily is slanted against the patterning of the hand-dyed background.

COLOR TALK

The flowers are stitched in Polyneon embroidery thread (by Madeira), with bright yellows and oranges toned down by purples, plums, and browns.

The leaf's curve gives it a sense of movement. Green and brown stitching follow the curve.

Japanese Lunch for Three, 16" × 42",
by Ellen Anne Eddy, 2008; owned by Kathy Kerestes

I love these fantasy flowers. My garden has Japanese beetles each year, and I'm torn between appreciating their beauty and dealing with their ravenous hunger. They chew through everything. I made a vine with these fabulous flowers, which are not something I found in nature but which are naturally lovely. Vivid flower stitching gives a perfect counterpoint to the much more quiet stitching on the beetles.

Planning Flowers from Elements 83

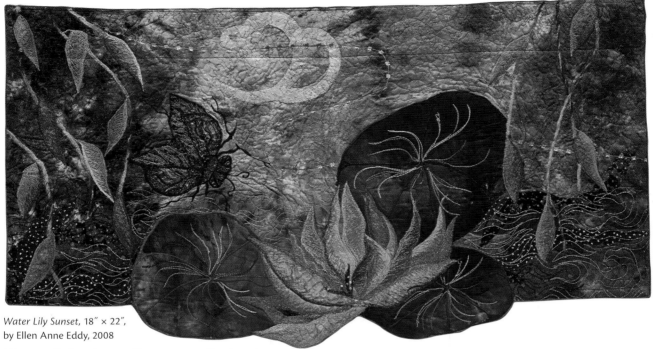

Water Lily Sunset, 18″ × 22″,
by Ellen Anne Eddy, 2008

This water lily floats in a pond between two willow branches.
The petals of the water lily echo the same dye colors that
create the sunset.

Daylily Dance, 60″ × 40″, by Ellen Anne Eddy, 2011

This is a Jazzed abstract piece. I love the notion of nature breaking through the background fabric. I started with 3½-yard panels of fabric that have light sources dyed into them. Then I created gray sidewalk strips to make a garden enclosure. C shapes create the daylilies, bell shapes make the vining flowers, and blue daisylike loop flowers weave through the piece. Of course, the flowers break out of their garden space to fill the room with their blooms. It's what gardens do.

Three-Point Landing, 36″ × 50″, by Ellen Anne Eddy, 2003

I love this wild-eyed dragonfly looking for a place to land. It's a pretty delicate maneuver to land exactly on a lily pad. The blue and purple complementary stitching makes the yellow daylilies more exciting; these flowers glow against the red-orange background. This quilt's colors span the entire color wheel.

Planning Flowers from Elements　85

Daylily Pond, 54" × 54", by Ellen Anne Eddy, 2001; owned by Deborah Lara

My dear friend Susan Hecker gave me a bucket of daylilies when I moved to Porter, Indiana. I put them along a pathway in early fall and forgot them until they rocketed into bloom in July. Susan died of cancer several years after that. Her daylilies remind me of her courage and her heart, both enormous. This quilt was made with her in mind. All kinds of orange sheers went into these daylilies. Orange is a color that goes in and out of fashion in waves, and sheers follow the fashion market. There are periods when you just can't find them, so I buy orange sheers religiously when I see them.

FLOWER STUDIES: S-Shaped Flowers

The S's of these petals fit gently into each other in so many flowers—sunflowers, poinsettias, and many other saucer-shaped flowers.

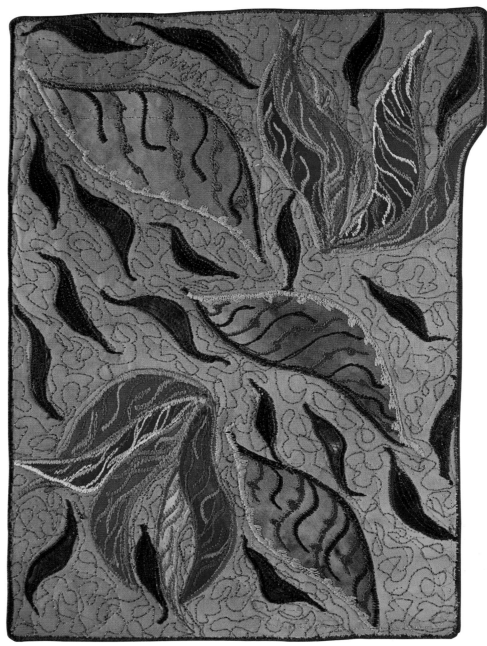

Jazzed: Floating S Flowers, 11″ × 14″, by Ellen Anne Eddy, 2010

The same S shapes that make the petals also make the leaves and the smaller purple background elements. Bright green garnet stitches edge the leaves.

S-Shaped Flowers: *Daffodil*

Grocery stores really know how to take our collective pulse. In late February, they put buckets of daffodils at the checkout counter. Who can resist? In the language of flowers, daffodils are a request for affection returned.

Photo by Ellen Anne Eddy

COMPONENTS

- **Petals:** 6 bulky S shapes (Some ornamentals have more or fewer.)
- **Center:** Bell-shaped cup
- **Leaves:** Narrow sword shapes
- **Stems:** Curved down at the top

COLOR TALK

The petals are stitched in every bright yellow thread I own. Dark purple and blue squiggles create the petal's fold. The cup is stitched in bright oranges and accentuated in a ruffled edge stitch. The inner cup is revealed with a swirling straight-stitch garnet stitch.

Daffodil leaves sometimes fold. They are stitched both ways here. Straight stitching down the center gives a sense of the fold without being overwhelming.

COMPOSITION

Unstitched version of *Daffodil Flower Study*— This daffodil is seen from a three-quarter view at eye level. Petals make up the saucer shape, while the cup is a bell stitched into dimension.

S-Shaped Flowers: *Lily*

It's no surprise that lilies represent loyalty. They come back year after year with great faithfulness. One of my lilies was planted by the woman who lived in my house 50 years ago. Lilies are dedicated to St. Mary and always show up at Easter.

Photo by Ellen Anne Eddy

COMPONENTS

- **Petals:** 6–8 S shapes, front ones cut in half

- **Leaves:** Thin, wavy, branching out of the stem

- **Stems:** Straight, stiff

- **Viewpoint:** Eye level from the front

STITCHING SENSE

Lily petals usually have stripes. I used a gentle, pale green line and two rows of pink garnet stitching to create the stripes.

Lily leaves are narrow, elongated horizontal fronds that go out on either side from the stiff stem. Rows of slanted outline stitches make perfect lily leaves.

COMPOSITION

Unstitched version of *Lily Flower Study*— The lily's cup is formed from petals meeting at the stem. The petals are cut with a curve to echo the cup shape.

S-Shaped Flowers: *Poinsettia*

Early South American cultures saw poinsettias as symbols of purity. Today, the December birth flower symbolizes good cheer and success and is said to bring wishes of mirth and celebration. No wonder we give them at Christmas!

Poinsettias are a saucer-shaped flower with leaves and petals that are almost the same shape. The center has a ring of tiny yellow flowers.

Silk flower poinsettia—While I was taking my pictures, it was the wrong time of year for poinsettias. Not to worry, thanks to silk blooms that are always available.

Photo by Ellen Anne Eddy

COMPONENTS

- **Petals:** 6 bulky S shapes
- **Center:** Small modified-circle flowers
- **Leaves:** Bulky S shapes
- **Stems:** Straight
- **Viewpoint:** From above

COLOR TALK

Deep reds and purples contrast with the brighter shades of red and orange that delineate the petals. The centers are simple threadwork in bright yellow.

The light hand-dyed cheesecloth adds texture and color contrast to the deeper veining and outlining on the leaf.

COMPOSITION

Unstitched version of *Poinsettia Flower Study*— I chose all kinds of brocades for the petals and hand-dyed cheesecloth for the leaves.

S-Shaped Flowers: *Sunflowers*

No flower is as wild or rough as sunflowers. They're so unruly; it's like they've been playing in the yard and refuse to sit politely. No wonder Van Gogh loved to paint them. In the language of flowers, they represent loyalty.

This sunflower was a volunteer in my front yard. I don't ordinarily plant them in the front, but how do you say no to a sunflower?

Photo by Ellen Anne Eddy

COMPONENTS

- **Petals:** Many S shapes
- **Leaves:** Shield shapes with wavy edges ending in points
- **Stems:** Stiff, thick
- **Viewpoints:** Side view: gumdrop shape; top view: circle

COLOR TALK

To represent their wild character, I colored these sunflowers in yellows, oranges, purples, plums, and greens. The wonderful wiggle down the center creases the petal in the right place to give it depth.

Sunflower leaves can be huge. The edges wave and end at sharp, ragged points.

COMPOSITION

Unstitched version of *Sunflower Study*—The top and side views show petals made from brocades and all kinds of commercial laces, with centers made from hand-dyed cheesecloth.

Drawn to the Sun 2, 14″ × 14″, by Ellen Anne Eddy, 2003;
owned by Wendy Strummwauser

I've done a series of sunflower quilts. I love this one for the mouse who's
dropped by for lunch. What good is a garden that doesn't feed your
neighbors? Machine beading adds texture to the center. The leaf, stitched
separately on cheesecloth and dissolvable stabilizer, adds dimensionality.

FLOWER STUDIES: Spiral-Shaped Flowers

Spiral shapes show up in spring ferns and make fabulous flower centers. They also create the best roses. Although a rose petal isn't spiral shaped, the spiral does echo how rose petals are spirally placed within the flower. In fabric, the spiral shape carries that illusion into the heart of a rose. Peonies, begonias, and gardenias also are arranged as spirals.

Jazzed: Spiraled, 11″ × 14″, by Ellen Anne Eddy, 2010

Spirals are a shape in motion. Dancing and interlocked across the surface, they make a bright floral display. The cool purple-blue spirals act as shadows of the hot orange-red-yellow elements. A strip of purple stitching on the inside of the spiral pops the shape dimensionally.

Spiral-Shaped Flowers: *Rose*

Roses are the heart of the language of flowers. Red roses are for love, yellow for friendship, pink for affection, and black for death.

My Hansa rosebush has huge thorns and an amazing flush of bright pink flowers that smell mildly like cloves. It blooms in June and September.

Hansa rose
Photo by Ellen Anne Eddy

COMPONENTS

- **Petals:** Multiple spirals in varied sizes
- **Leaves:** Wavy shield shapes
- **Stems:** Vine stems: delicate curves; other stems: stiff, stalky

STITCHING SENSE

Spirals with points accentuated in stitching make the petals appear to fold into the center. Spiral curlicues give a windblown feel to the petals. Both warm and cool pinks and reds create a centered pink shade for the flower.

Leaves are detailed with a zigzag stitch straight out to the side from the center stem. The angle makes the stitch more delicate.

COMPOSITION

Unstitched version of *Rose Flower Study*—Spirals make this rose in shades of red and pink cheesecloth, with leaves in hand-dyed cotton. A small lime spiral is at the center.

Yellow Rose, 9″ × 15″, by Ellen Anne Eddy, 2008
owned by Mary R. Baumer

The spiraled ends of these rose petals almost unwind the flower, as if it's at the end of its display. I'm always surprised at how far the color range of roses can stretch. Although orange and purple shade this flower, it's still very yellow. The brightest color usually defines the shade.

Butterfly and Rose, 15″ × 13″, by Ellen Anne Eddy, 2010

Wherever you have roses, you have butterflies. They are always in concert together. So the blue butterfly needed to be part of this rose quilt.

Planning Flowers from Elements   95

FLOWER STUDIES: Teardrop Flowers

Teardrop shapes, like S shapes, fit into each other. This shape creates great fantasy flowers, as well as all kinds of blooming trees, such as cherry, plum, pear, and wisteria. Wavier versions make many bulb and bloom flowers, such as nasturtiums, hollyhocks, poppies, snapdragon, bee balm, and tulips.

Jazzed: Tear Drop Vine, 11″ × 14″, by Ellen Anne Eddy, 2010

TEARDROP FLOWERS: *Wisteria*

I tried so hard to grow wisteria because they're so wonderfully purple! I did a great job of growing a wisteria vine that eventually knocked down its support—but never bloomed. So wisteria has to be a plant I visit in my travels and my dreams. In the language of flowers, wisteria offers welcome.

Photo by Lauren Strach

COMPONENTS

- **Petals:** Many teardrop shapes
- **Leaves:** Not out when it's in bloom
- **Vine:** Strong branch shape

COMPOSITION

Unstitched version of *Wisteria Flower Study*— Teardrop shapes fit into each other on the vine, creating a ribbon of blossoms.

COLOR TALK

Couched rows of novelty yarn add color and woody texture to the branch (see Machine Couching, page 29).

Warm green-gold accents set off the very cool blues and purples in the blossoms.

TEARDROP FLOWERS: *Bee Balm*

These late-June, early-July flowers are firecrackers against a summer green yard. They come in a color range from hot pink to bluish red. Part of the mint family, bee balm is a component in many perfumes and Earl Grey tea. In the language of flowers, bee balm represents compassion and sweet virtues.

Photo by Ellen Anne Eddy

COMPONENTS

- ■ **Petals:** Many elongated teardrop shapes
- ■ **Center:** Oval
- ■ **Leaves:** Wavy shield shapes with small, ragged points
- ■ **Stem:** Straight, square
- ■ **Viewpoint:** From above

STITCHING SENSE

The flowers are large masses of petals springing from the center. As the bloom matures, the petals fall out, and more of the center is displayed. I used beading to accentuate the flower's seedpod center.

The leaves are outlined with dark thread that matches the fabric. Lighter green thread accentuates veins and highlights.

COMPOSITION

Unstitched version of *Bee Balm Flower Study*—Pink and red cheesecloth creates a good color base for the stitching.

TEARDROP FLOWERS: *Tulip*

I love when my tulips bloom because they turn my yard into masses of bright red and yellow. In the language of flowers, tulips are a declaration of love. For me, they mean spring is done teasing and has finally arrived.

Photo by Ellen Anne Eddy

COMPONENTS

- **Petals:** 6 wavy teardrops joined at the bottom to make a cup-shaped flower. As the blooms develop, the petals spread wider until they drop off.
- **Leaves:** Fat sword shapes
- **Stems:** Straight or gently curved

COMPOSITION

Unstitched version of *Tulip Flower Study*— This tulip is viewed from the side after it has been in bloom several days. The petals have started to open.

COLOR TALK

Purple stitching shades the petal, making the flower's center ridge pop. The back petal is in darker shades to make it recede.

Lines of wavy stitches echo the lines running down the leaf.

TEARDROP FLOWERS: *Nasturtium*

This low-growing ground cover is a newcomer to my garden. I love its flaming bright blooms among the leaves. It's also fabulous in a salad. In the language of flowers, it represents conquest, victory in battle, maternal love, and patriotism—all ferocious, but lovely, things.

Photo by Ellen Anne Eddy

COMPONENTS

- **Petals:** 6 wavy teardrop shapes
- **Leaves:** Round, divided in the center
- **Stems:** Curved, vinelike

COMPOSITION

Unstitched version of *Nasturtium Flower Study*—These petals, viewed from above, fit into a blazing red whorl.

COLOR TALK

This cup-shaped flower has a bright yellow center accentuated by machine beading.

Pale yellow and green stitched stars detail the leaves.

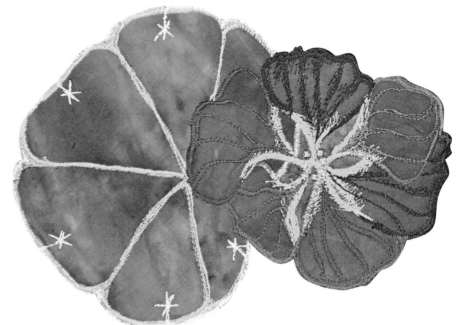

TEARDROP FLOWERS: *Iris*

A clump of irises blooms in my front yard. In June, irises turn the whole yard to blues and purples. In the language of flowers, they represent loyalty and faith.

Photo by Lauren Strach

COMPONENTS

- **Petals:** 4 teardrop petals joined at the point; 2 side petals lean out
- **Bud:** Rice shape
- **Leaves:** Slightly curved sword shapes
- **Stem:** Bud shape on top

COMPOSITION

Unstitched version of *Iris Flower Study*— This iris is seen from the side and slightly from below.

COLOR TALK

The top petal of an iris has a slight saucer rim, which is made to pop with the lighter yellow stitching. The three lower petals are curved under by the darker brown and purple stitching and given weight and depth with orange highlights.

The leaves are minimally stitched. A slanted outline stitch down the leaf's center texturizes the rib.

Snail's Pace, 25″ × 52″, by Ellen Anne Eddy, 2006; owned by Nancy Turbs

The irises are a soaring contrast to the snails. The snails were made from a fabulous fabric with embroidered circles. All they needed were little snail heads. It was fun to place something that stretches so high against something on a completely different plane in the same world.

Duet, 50″ × 44″, by Ellen Anne Eddy, 2005; owned by Paula Donn

Irises are almost swamp plants, best planted in bright sun by the water. These irises are teardrop shapes, with the top blossom rimmed to create dimensionality.

This fantasy vine makes a chain of teardrops that sweep across the quilt's surface.

Planning Flowers from Elements 103

Midnight Stroll, 9″ × 19″, by Ellen Anne Eddy, 2010

I'm not sure what blossom makes her little parasol; I only know I love it. Small teardrops cut from sheers and lamé join to make a lovely flower. Stitching fashions the stem.

Wisteria Pond, 24″ × 36″, by Ellen Anne Eddy, 2006

The hand-dyed fabric in the background had pink inclusions that suggested wisteria flowers. So I added tear-shaped blossoms in loops, draping from the branches and floating in the pond.

Nestling Ladies, 20″ × 47″, by Ellen Anne Eddy, 2006

I love water birds and swamps. This bittern is in her nest, which is surrounded by lady slippers. I can't grow lady slippers in my yard, but they grow beautifully in my studio. The lady slippers are made from Crystalina fiber, which I fused to make a sheer surface. I stitched them with polyester embroidery threads in purples and browns. The effect is that of a silk slipper, exactly right for this glowing flower. The leaves are cut from hand-dyed cheesecloth to add to their ghostly quality.

Wisteria Afternoon, 22″ × 13″, by Ellen Anne Eddy, 2010

Wisteria droops gracefully above this pond at sunset, framing the water in blossoms and branches. Both the blossoms and the moth are created from teardrop shapes. The difference between a moth and a dragonfly is mostly in the body shape and antenna. The body shape for a dragonfly is elongated, while a moth's antennae are closer and much hairier.

Detail of *Snail's Pace* (page 102)—Both the irises and the butterfly are teardrop shapes. The butterfly's blue-lace wings are almost triangles, and the irises are four teardrops with ruffled edges.

Creatures in My Garden

This is a book about flowers. But dragonflies, moths, snails, bunnies, frogs, owls, and all other sorts of creatures inhabit my gardens, both in my backyard and in my studio. Most of the creatures in my quilts are fanciful figures, with bodies and wings made in brocades and laces of improbable colors. Some of them are made of stitching alone. The same machine embroidery stitches I use to outline, shade, texturize, and fill the flowers can be used to ornament the creatures in a variety of metallic and polyester threads.

For ideas on creating creatures to add to your quilts, look at photographs, encyclopedias, and children's coloring books. To learn more about designing without a pattern, see Observation (pages 7–10).

Try to simplify your design shapes. For example, all bugs have the same basic elements—head, thorax, and abdomen, with wings attached between head and thorax, front legs pointed forward, and two sets of back legs facing backward. I elongate the bug legs to add direction and to give the bugs personality.

Detail of *Wisteria Pond* (page 104)—This fish is embroidered with sizes 5–8 perle cotton and metallic threads. These luscious, thick threads go through the bobbin in an adjusted bobbin case and are stitched from the back. The top threads are 40-weight polyester embroidery threads.

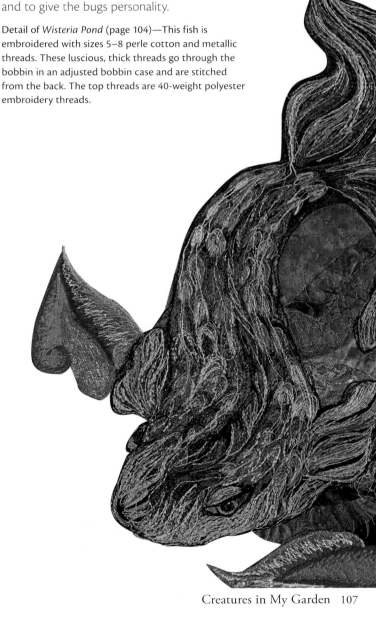

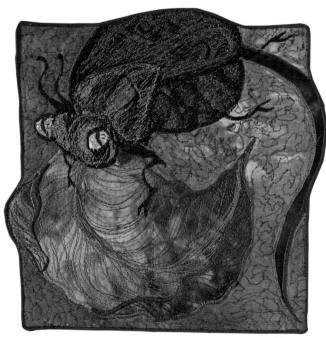

Bugged Beetle, 10″ × 10″, by Ellen Anne Eddy, 2006; owned by Betty Knight Davis

All bugs have three basic body parts. You can arrange them at different angles to show the bug's movement.

CREATURES: *Dragonfly Study*

I so often add these insects to my garden quilts; it seemed unfair not to show them. The bugs in my garden are my co-gardeners. They're as involved in the garden as I am, sometimes more so. Certainly they float through with purpose and passion. The same shapes that make a dragonfly can be used for butterflies and other bugs.

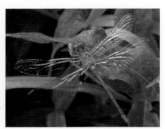

Photo by Lauren Strach

COMPONENTS

- **Wings:** 2 larger teardrop shapes; 2 smaller teardrop shapes
- **Body:** Elongated
- **Eyes:** Oval cut in half
- **Viewpoint:** From the top

STITCHING SENSE

Straight stitching in metallic thread makes the veins in the wings. I recolored the eyes with bright gold sliver thread when the original green didn't give enough contrast.

COMPOSITION

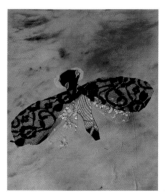

Unstitched version of *Dragonfly Study*— Wild commercial laces make the wings. Stitching will define the color, but the laces make a nice textural base.

All Time Is Spiral in a Garden

Seasons are measured by the flowers that bud and bloom year after year in a set order. Time is spiral in a garden.

The seasons wheel by, marked by tulips and cherry blossoms, violets and irises, lilies and phlox. The blooms come back each year somewhat the same yet always somehow different. The spiral always comes around. The studio garden spirals as well.

I weary of roses and can't leave the hostas alone until it's time to do clematis. It's a more chaotic system, but just as changeable. Flowers bloom in gardens under my hands and my machine. I'm hoping your studio garden, like mine, is full of wildflowers, lovely weeds, cultured blooms, and joy.

All Time Is Spiral in a Garden, 30″ × 37″, by Ellen Anne Eddy, 2008

About the Author

Photo by Mary Beth Fladlung
Ellen Anne Eddy

Ellen has spent most of her life teaching, writing, or working with fabric, and now she's come to a point where all occupations blend. She grew up in Streator, Illinois, went to college at Knox College in Galesburg, Illinois, and did some graduate studies at Boston State University.

She began quilting in response to a gift from a neighbor, Mary Annis, who saved Ellen's grandmother's quilt top from one of her mother's cleaning fits. Mary had the top quilted and gave it to Ellen once she was grown. The gift was such an inspiration that Ellen has been quilting ever since.

The National Quilt Museum in Paducah, Kentucky, acquired one her quilts, *Dancing in the Light*, in June 2010. She has won numerous prizes at quilt shows nationally and internationally.

Her first book, *Thread Magic: The Enchanted World of Ellen Anne Eddy*, has proved to be a classic text on free-motion stitching and fiber art. See Resources (page 111).

She dyes all of the fabric and some of the embroidery thread for her own projects and has a variety of fabric and thread for sale on her website. She has written a book called *Ellen Anne Eddy's Dye Day Workbook* about her unusual dyeing method—a measureless intuitive process. With her technique she creates the extraordinary landscape backgrounds for her quilts, as well as fabrics with spots, lines, graduated colors, streaks, textures, and spots for the appliquéd elements of her quilts. Ellen's publishing company, Thread Magic Studio Press, has also published several of her other books, including *Tigrey Leads the Parade, Dragonfly Sky, A Ladybug's Garden, Quick and Easy Machine Binding Techniques*, and *The Town of Torper and the Very Vulgar Day Lily*. For information about Ellen's products, see Resources (page 111).

She has written for numerous fiber arts publications, including *Quilting Arts, American Quilter, Quilters Newsletter, Threads*, and *Fiberarts*.

Ellen currently teaches a series of fiber art courses called Thread Magic for quilt guilds and conferences across the country. The courses cover many free-motion machine-embroidery techniques. She also teaches Dye Day workshops at her studio.

To schedule a workshop or learn where she is teaching next, see her website: www.ellenanneeddy.com.

To learn more about her current projects, see her blog: www.ellenanneeddy.blogspot.com.

Also by Ellen Anne Eddy:

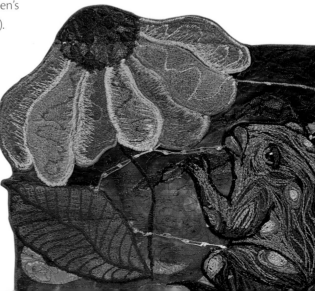

Resources

For Ellen Anne Eddy's hand-dyed fabrics, threads, embroidery kits, *Ellen Anne Eddy's Dye Day Workbook*, and other books and products:

Thread Magic Studio Press
125 Franklin Street
Porter, IN 46304
219-921-0885
www.ellenanneeddy.com

For other fine books:

C&T Publishing, Inc.
800-284-1114
www.ctpub.com;
www.ctmediaservices.com (C&T's professional photography services)
Thread Magic: The Enchanted World of Ellen Anne Eddy; Fast, Fun & Easy Fabric Dyeing (by Lynn Koolish); *Fabric Dyer's Dictionary* (by Linda Johansen); and many others

For fabrics and other quilting supplies:

The Cotton Patch
925-284-1177
www.quiltusa.com

For fusible webbing and stabilizers:

Brewer Quilting and Sewing Supplies
800-676-6543 or 630-820-5965
www.brewersewing.com
Hydro-Stick, 505 Spray and Fix, AquaFilm Wash-Away Topping
Wholesale only. For retail sales, contact your local sewing and embroidery supply center.

Pellon
800-223-5275
www.pellonideas.com
Stitch-n-Tear

The Warm Company
425-248-2424
www.warmcompany.com
Steam-A-Seam 2

For threads:

Madeira USA-Headquarters
800-225-3001
www.madeirausa.com
Madeira Metallic Supertwist and Polyneon threads

Sulky of America
800-874-4115
www.sulky.com
Sliver threads

Superior Threads
800-499-1777
www.superiorthreads.com
Metallic, polyester trilobal, and monofilament threads

YLI Corporation
803-985-3100
www.ylicorp.com
Monofilament threads

For other materials and tools:

Bear Thread Designs
281-462-0661
www.bearthreaddesigns.com
The Appliqué Pressing Sheet

Bernina of America, Inc.
www.berninausa.com/product_search-n25-sUS.html
Bernina Buttonhole Foot #3/3c

Fire Mountain Gems
800-355-2137
www.firemountaingems.com
Seed beads

Prym Consumer USA Inc.
www.dritz.com
Sewers Aid lubricant for thread

Schamber Quilts
928-474-9143
www.sharonschamber.com
Quilt Halo

Textura Trading Company
877-839-8872
www.texturatrading.com
Angelina and Crystalina fibers

Great Titles and Products *from* C&T PUBLISHING

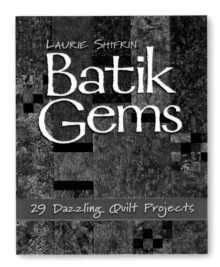

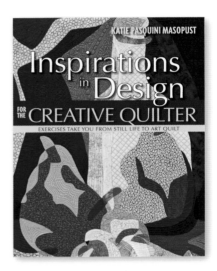

Available at your local retailer or **www.ctpub.com** *or* **800-284-1114**

For a list of other fine books from C&T Publishing, visit our website
to view our catalog online.

C&T PUBLISHING, INC.

P.O. Box 1456
Lafayette, CA 94549
800-284-1114

Email: ctinfo@ctpub.com
Website: www.ctpub.com

C&T Publishing's professional photography services are now available to
the public. Visit us at www.ctmediaservices.com.

Tips and Techniques can be found at www.ctpub.com > Consumer
Resources > Quiltmaking Basics: Tips & Techniques for Quiltmaking & More

For quilting supplies:

COTTON PATCH

1025 Brown Ave.
Lafayette, CA 94549
Store: 925-284-1177
Mail order: 925-283-7883

Email: CottonPa@aol.com
Website: www.quiltusa.com

Note: Fabrics shown may not be currently available, as fabric
manufacturers keep most fabrics in print for only a short time.